❧ home ❧
brewing

A Practical Guide to Crafting Your
Own Beer, Wine, and Cider

home

brewing

A Practical Guide to Crafting Your Own Beer, Wine, and Cider

Kevin Forbes

FOX CHAPEL
PUBLISHING

First published in the United Kingdom by Arcturus Publishing Limited, 2010.
First published in North America in 2012, revised, by Fox Chapel Publishing, 1970 Broad Street, East Petersburg, PA 17520.

ISBN 978-1-56523-701-8

Library of Congress Cataloging-in-Publication Data

Forbes, Kevin.
 Home brewing / Kevin Forbes.
    p. cm.
 Includes index.
 ISBN 978-1-56523-701-8
 1. Brewing--Amateurs' manuals. I. Title.
 TP570.F67 2011
 641.87'3--dc23
                         2011024125

To learn more about the other great books from Fox Chapel Publishing, or to find a retailer near you, call toll-free 800-457-9112 or visit us at *www.FoxChapelPublishing.com*.

Note to Authors: We are always looking for talented authors to write new books. Please send a brief letter describing your idea to Acquisition Editor, 1970 Broad Street, East Petersburg, PA 17520.

Printed in China
First printing

Because working with fermenting liquids and other materials inherently includes the risk of injury and damage, this book cannot guarantee that using the recipes in this book is safe for everyone. For this reason, this book is sold without warranties or guarantees of any kind, expressed or implied, and the publisher and the author disclaim any liability for any injuries, losses, or damages caused in any way by the content of this book or the reader's use of the ingredients needed to complete the recipes presented here. The publisher and the author urge all readers to thoroughly review each project and to understand the effects of all ingredients before starting any recipe.

CONTENTS

INTRODUCTION

The satisfaction of producing excellent beers, ciders and wines at home can be had by anyone with a little bit of effort. A shortcut is to buy one of the many kits available, but if you want more fun and a superior result, follow the guidance and many recipes in this book.

Many people enjoy cooking at home and perhaps even making up their own recipes. Those who care about what they eat tend to care about how food is produced, and if they have a large enough garden and the time they will often grow their own vegetables.

But comparatively few people take up brewing and winemaking, even though the perfect accompaniment to a home-cooked meal made from garden produce would be a drink also derived from home-grown crops. Perhaps this is because the ingredients and processes that go into making your own beers and wines are not visually appealing. A large bucket of brown, foamy liquid can't compete in the looks stakes with an oozing cherry pie straight from the oven. But it can hold its own in all other respects, especially flavor and goodness.

Here are just a few of the excellent reasons you should create your own drinks (alcholic and non-alcoholic) at home:

- You can make drinks with pure and high-quality ingredients. The drinks can, if you wish, be free from unnecessary sugars, preservatives and other chemicals.

- You can make drinks to organic standards.

- You can adapt recipes to your own taste.

- You can save money.

- You can enjoy the satisfaction of creating something individual.

It is advisable to start with easy, simple drinks, then learn to build your skills at your own pace before moving on to more complex recipes. Your first batch of beer or wine is highly unlikely to be the finest you ever produce. Most home brewers find they get better over time. The aim at all stages of your development is to produce something that you enjoy drinking.

Beers

BREWING BEERS

Man has been brewing beer since the dawn of civilization, and it is still the third most widely-consumed beverage after water and tea. You can easily produce your own high quality beer at home and make it cheaper than it would be to purchase low-quality beer, mass-produced in a factory.

There are those that claim that it is not just coincidence that beer has been around since the dawn of civilization, but that beer was the catalyst for neolithic hunter/gatherers to have reason to settle in one place, start farming and form organized communities. Cereal was among the first and most important crops, and making beer was an important use of this crop (although some academics claim that making bread was the main purpose for this farming).

There is something very rewarding about brewing your own beer. Perhaps it is because it is not just any beer, but one that you have designed and created yourself. Brewing beer is an ideal hobby for people with busy lives as it really does not take too much time to create a really drinkable beer. Home brewing is an interesting hobby and a rewarding one as well, and what greater reward do you need than beer?

There are many and varied reasons for brewing your own beer, for example:

- You can save money—most brews can be made more cheaply than the equivalent commercial beers.
- Enjoy the challenge! Making beer from kits is easy but there is a skill and art in brewing a beer from the raw ingredients.
- Make the type of beers you want to drink. It is very easy to find lagers but in some areas not so easy to find mild ales, bottle conditioned ales or trappist beers, so make your own!
- Make beers to your taste. Choose how hoppy or malty you wish the beer to taste.
- Make beer the strength you wish.

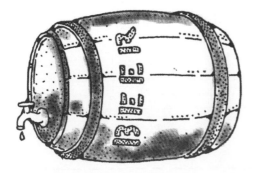

KITS OR MASHES

There are a number of ways to brew beer at home but before going through the options let's look at the basic brewing process broken down into four stages:

1. Mashing: The soaking of ground malted barley in hot water, producing sweet wort.
2. Sweet wort is then mixed with hops, producing hopped wort.
3. Yeast is added to the hopped wort mixture and it is left to ferment.
4. The beer matures in bottles or kegs with sugar or carbon dioxide added to increase carbonation.

BREWING FROM A KIT

Undoubtedly the easiest way to start brewing is to use one of the many kits available. Essentially, these beer kits are concentrated hopped worts, so in effect steps 1 and 2 are done for you. These concentrates are produced in the same way a brewer would, but after the hops are added some excess liquid is evaporated under vacuum at low temperatures to preserve the delicate flavors, then the concentrate is pasteurized and canned. To continue the brewing process at home, all that is necessary is to dilute the concentrated wort back to its original density, ferment and then bottle or keg it.

Sometimes extra hops are included to restore aroma lost during production. Some cheaper kits require that you add a large amount of sugar to the concentrate before fermentation. These cheaper kits are alright if your budget is tight or if you are just starting out on your new hobby, but will not, in most cases, produce beers to the same quality as the more expensive, no sugar, all grain kits.

The advantage of brewing from a kit is the ease of obtaining all the ingredients you need. The recipe is taken care of for you and less equipment and space is needed than for other methods.

BREWING FROM MALT EXTRACT

This method is more complex than using a kit. The malt extract concentrate does not contain hops and when diluted and heated gives you the equivalent of sweet wort. You then add the hop flavor by adding a muslin bag (sparge bag) containing the hops to the sweet wort, for around 20 minutes towards the end of the heating process. The resulting hopped wort is then fermented and bottled or kegged.

HALF OR PARTIAL MASHES

Half mashes are a halfway house between the concentrated malt kits and a full mash.

The sweet wort is made from a combination of specialty grains soaked in hot water and malt extract.

The advantages of partial over full mash are that you don't require quite so much space, equipment or skill. The advantages of partial over a malt extract brew is that you have more control over the finished beer.

BREWING A FULL MASH

At the other end of the scale of complexity from the homebrew kit is the full mash. There certainly is craft and skill in brewing a full mash and the effort involved in acquiring these skills and brewing full mashes will reward you with the satisfaction of brewing beers as good, if not better than, commercial breweries.

To produce a full mash, first of all you need a grist. This is a mix of crushed, dry grains that are mixed together before mashing. Typically, the major portion of this grist would be pale malt with maybe a small amount of crystal malt. Other widely used grains are wheat, corn and dark roasted malts.

The grist is then mashed, i.e. it is soaked in hot water for an hour or two. The purpose of mashing is to convert the starch in the grist (which isn't fermentable by brewer's yeast) into sugar (which is).

The mash is then sparged. Sparging is rinsing the mashed grains with water to get as much sugar out of the grain as is possible.

After sparging, the hops are added to the wort and the hopped wort is boiled for an hour or so. This boiling stage extracts flavor from the hops, sterilizes and helps clear protein debris from the wort.

The wort is then cooled to the appropriate temperature so the yeast can be added. Fermentation will take around 10 to 14 days.

When the resulting brew is bottled or kegged, a small amount of sugar is added to start a secondary fermentation. This is to provide carbon dioxide gas to create condition and promote head formation.

EQUIPMENT

CLEAN ALL EQUIPMENT!

Every surface that touches your beer during the brewing process should be clean and free from soap residues. Without proper cleaning, surface build up may harbor bacteria and other unwanted organisms. All stains, dirt and other visible contaminants must be removed from your brewing equipment. Unscented washing up liquid will do the job but make sure all detergent is thoroughly rinsed off.

Sanitize

Strictly speaking, the sterilizing done by home brewers is in fact sanitizing, as we don't completely kill off all the microorganisms on our equipment, but simply reduce them to a harmless level. After cleaning, all equipment that comes into contact with your beer after it has been boiled must be sanitized. It is not necessary to sanitize equipment that contacts your wort before and during the boil, as the process of boiling will sterilize both the beer and the boiling pot. There are a number of chemicals you can use to sanitize your equipment and there is more information on these later in the equipment section.

ESSENTIAL EQUIPMENT

As with many hobbies and pastimes there are some essential things you need and then there are some bits of kit that are useful but not strictly necessary. You need a lot more equipment for brewing mashes than you do brewing from a kit.

The bare minimum equipment for brewing from a kit would be a large pot, long handled spoon, fermenting vessel, airlock and bung, siphon tube, bottles, caps and capper and sanitizer/cleaner.

When brewing from malt extract, add to the above a large boiling pan and a sparge bag. When brewing mashes you will also need a water boiler and sparger. A hydrometer and thermometer are not essential for even full mash brewing, but are very worthwhile investments.

Sanitizing chemicals

Sanitizers are not, stricly speaking, equipment, but are certainly essential. Detergent will do for cleaning equipment but this will not sanitize. There are a number of chemicals that will kill most of the microorganisms found on homebrew equipment.

Probably the easiest to obtain is unscented bleach. You can use it at a rate of 6 tablespoons of bleach to 5 quarts (5 liters) of water. After using bleach at this rate of dilution be sure to rinse carefully afterward.

Some brewers use bleach as a no-rinse sanitizer. This is not recommended because you need to be very exact about dilution rates and take into account the amount of active ingredients, which varies widely. You also need to know the pH of the water used to dilute the bleach as it affects the strength of the solution.

Another option is a proprietary homebrew cleaner, which is basically a chlorinated caustic powder that can be found at your local homebrew supplier. These cleaners also have to be rinsed off before the equipment is used.

No-rinse sanitizers, as the name suggests, are solutions that can be used to sanitize equipment without the need to rinse afterward. This is either because they don't leave any residue except water on the equipment, or because the residue that remains will not taint or harm the beer or anyone consuming it.

Pot

A pot (the larger the better) will do for brewing from a kit because you only need boil 5 to 11 quarts (5 to 10 liters) of water. However, an electric water boiler/urn would be useful, as the cold water you use would be sterilized if you pre-boiled it.

Large capacity water boiler

When brewing mashes you really need to be able to boil about 20 quarts (19 liters) of liquid at a time. A water boiler (the sort used in the catering trade to fill teapots) with a capacity of 26 quarts, about 32 quarts to the brim (25 liters, about 30 liters to the brim) would be ideal. As well as catering boilers you can also buy from homebrew shops, purpose-made devices that act as both mash tun and boiler and some can be used as fermentation buckets as well. It should have a fine mesh stainless steel false bottom just above the draw off tap, to prevent the crushed grains from blocking it. These units enable you to set and automatically maintain an accurate mash temperature throughout the mashing period. Some sort of insulation blanket would be beneficial.

Insulated chest

Large insulated camping chests/coolers can be used for the mashing process if they are capable of withstanding temperatures of 185°F (85°C). These chests can be used as they come, but many brewers customize and improve them. This mainly consists of improving the insulation, adding taps and some filtration above the tap. When using these chests pre-heat them by filling with water that is 176°F (80°C) and add the grain when the water is 167°F (75°C). This should mean the temperature of the mash will stabilize at an ideal 149°F (65°C) for 2 hours.

Sparge bag

Also known as a grain bag that, as the name suggests, contains the crushed grains. Keeping them in a bag while you mash has many advantages including keeping the grain suspended off, out of the way of the boiler element.

Sparger

Sparging is the process of rinsing the grains after mashing. This requires a large amount (usually 20 quarts, 19 liters) of hot water that can be dispensed quickly in a fine spray. You can use a well-insulated plastic bucket or barrel with a tap on the bottom, to which is attached a hose with a fine shower head.

Fermenting vessel

Assuming you're making 24 quarts (23 liters), you'll need something that holds at least 26 quarts (25 liters) but preferably 29 to 35 quarts (27 to 33 liters). This will allow for some foaming during fermentation. Even if your first brew is less than 24 quarts (23 liters) still go for a 29- to 35-quart (27- to 33-liter) bucket as this is a more useful size for future use.

A good, purpose-made fermenting bucket will be designed to be easy to clean and made from special, food grade plastic. They will come with either a screwtop or snap-on lid. Some buckets come with graduated markings to aid the measuring of liquids. Handles are useful for ease of carrying. A fitted tap is very useful, otherwise you will need to siphon the brew off the yeast. Also useful, would be a hole bored in the lid—standard demijohn size rubber bung—for fitting an airlock.

Glass containers are another possible option for fermentation vessels. Glass fermenters are known as carboys or demijohns. In the UK a demijohn holds 5 quarts (5 liters), and a carboy usually 25 quarts (24 liters); however, this varies widely throughout the brewing world. A 5-quart (5-liter) demijohn can be used for small batches and trial recipes but a carboy of 25 quarts (24 liters) is the most useful size. The disadvantages of glass containers include their fragility—it can be dangerous if they shatter while you are handling them. Glass containers don't come with a tap, therefore you have to siphon your brew off the yeast. Although the glass material is easier to clean than plastic, glass containers generally have openings that are too small to get your hands in. So to give any stubborn stains a good scrub, you will need to use bottlebrushes.

The main advantage of glass is that it is completely non-porous, making it easy to clean and sanitize. Glass is also preferred to plastic because the plastic is easily scratched and can harbor bacteria that is difficult to remove.

If the budget is really tight and you want a free fermenting bucket, try asking a local catering businesses if they have any large food grade containers they don't need.

Brewing spoon

You will need a brewing spoon. The spoon should be at least 18 in (45 cm) long and made out of either plastic or stainless steel.

Airlock

The airlock allows carbon dioxide to escape during fermentation and prevents air from entering the fermentation vessel, which may possibly contaminate the brew. The gas bubbling through the airlock gives an indication as to how hard the yeast is working.

Sometimes the water from the airlock is inadvertently drawn into the fermenter. If this water has not been sterilized there is a chance the brew may be contaminated by it. You can use pre-boiled cold water or some brewers use vodka in the fermentation lock to prevent contamination.

As well as an airlock you will probably need a suitable rubber stopper to seal the carboy/container.

Bottle/keg filling equipment

The transfer of beer must be done as smoothly as possible. If you have a tap on your fermenting bucket, a short length of tube from the tap would help cut down on foaming and therefore cut the risk of infection. You can improve further on this by using a bottle filler. This is also a tube that sticks on to the tap but it also has a valve at the bottom. This valve opens when you push the bottle up around it.

If you don't have a tap on your bucket you need a siphon tube or a jug to transfer your beer to bottles or kegs. If you use a siphon tube, a small tap on the filling end is invaluable for stopping flow while moving between bottles. A sediment trap (a long, rigid J-shaped tube) on the fermenting bucket end reduceS sediment pick-up. Also available is an auto siphon that has a small pump to start the flow.

Bottles

Kegs can be expensive, so most home brewers start by bottling their first beers.

Remember the amount of beer you brew will determine the number and size of the bottles you need. If you stick to one size of bottle it will make it easier to store them. The larger the size of bottle you use, the less work there will be in cleaning and filling them.

In the days of the returnable bottle it was much easier to obtain bottles suitable for homebrew because these were designed to be reusable. Now the vast majority of bottles are made to be used once only, consequently they are thinner and weaker.

You should still be able to gather a good supply of suitable bottles fairly easily. If you want to use pre-used glass bottles, go for those that have been used for ales that are bottle conditioned because the bottles must be made strong enough to cope with this. Sadly and inexplicably, bottle conditioned beers are not easy to find these days. So look for bottles that look strong, that feel chunky and heavy, these will generally be from premium quality beers. Do not use flimsy, light-weight bottles from cheap beers. Also don't be tempted to use screwtop wine bottles because these are not made to withstand the pressure of bottle conditioned beer.

The bottles should be made of brown glass, because brown tinted glass protects the beer against photochemistry, which may damage or alter the beer's qualities. Both sunlight and fluorescent light can interact with hop compounds in beer to produce a skunky aroma. Brown glass prevents the specific wavelength of light that is responsible for this reaction from reaching the beer (green glass offers only slightly better protection than clear glass).

This skunking reaction takes place after only a few minutes of exposure to sunlight. However, having said that, you can keep clear or green bottles in a dark cupboard or in a box and you won't need to worry about light damage. Also, filling one clear bottle in a batch allows you to watch the yeast settle and check color and clarity to aid you in judging when the beer is ready to drink.

If you can't get enough bottles try asking friends and family, raiding the local bottle bank or try requesting suitable bottles on the recycling notice board: http://www.freecycle.org.

If need be, new glass bottles can be obtained for little cost from homebrew suppliers.

> **IMPORTANT!**
> All glass bottles you use must be inspected carefully prior to use and any having damage or an imperfection must be discarded.

The plastic polyethylene terephthalate (PET) bottles that are used to contain fizzy drinks can be used for your homebrew and this option is gaining popularity among home brewers. Be sure to use bottles that have contained carbonated drinks and not those used for still water or cordials.

The advantages of using PET bottles include:
- They are a good option for those new to homebrewing.
- You will not have the danger of shattering glass bottles although PET bottles may explode under extreme pressure.
- No capper is needed.
- They all have screwtops and so are easily and quickly sealed.
- They are lightweight, this means they are easier to use and store and this also makes them a lot cheaper if you buy new via mail order.

Disadvantages of PET include:
- Traditionally good beer comes on draught or from a glass bottle. Beer from a plastic bottle just does not seem right.
- PET bottles are slightly porous to oxygen, which will eventually result in off flavors. Beer kept in PET bottles for up to 3

months should be fine but for longer-term storage, glass bottles would be preferable.

- Most fizzy drink bottles are clear, so you will need to store these in a dark cupboard. For brown PET bottles you need to use beer or cider bottles. You can find reasonable cider in brown PET bottles but most of the beer is undrinkable.

Bottle capper

Obviously this is not needed if you use screwtop PET bottles, but a good capper is essential for crown-capped glass bottles. The simple cappers that you use to hammer down caps on to bottles can be very awkward to use; there is a real knack to using them and a risk of damaging the bottles. Far better to invest in a twin lever or a bench capper.

IMPORTANT!
If you suspect you have damaged a bottle during the capping process, ditch the bottle, beer and all. Ingested glass is not good!

A good-quality twin lever capper makes light work of what can be a long and tedious task. Simply place a crown cap between the two handles, then place the crown cap over the beer bottle and push down on the handles. Continue pushing until the crown cap is firmly sealed around the mouth of the beer bottle. The problem with a twin lever capper is that it grips the bottle at the neck and this means it is not

possible to use them on some types of bottles with very short or bulbous necks.

A bench capper can be attached to a work surface (temporarily or permanently) and this leaves one hand free to hold the bottle. It can be used for just about any bottle up to 25 fl oz (750 ml) in size.

Plastic pressure barrel

Although initially more expensive than a collection of bottles, plastic pressure barrels do have many advantages. The most popular and easiest to obtain are the ones that hold 25 quarts (25 liters), which means there is only one container to clean and sterilize. Secondary fermentation can take place within the barrel and will safely cope with the pressure. The tap sits above the level of the sediment and the cap can, if required, have a carbon dioxide injector fitted.

Funnel

This is essential if you are using a carboy or any other type of fermenting vessel with a narrow neck.

Hydrometer

A hydrometer is a device used for measuring the density of a liquid. It is a long, thin, glass cylinder, weighted at the bottom. With the weighted end submerged in the liquid, the calibrated stem projects out of the liquid at a height determined by the density of that liquid. Readings from the hydrometer's calibrated markings are taken at the liquid's surface.

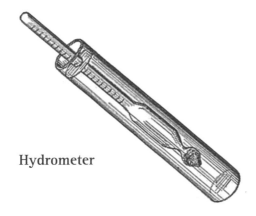

Hydrometer

With a hydrometer you can check the specific gravity (SG) of the beer (how dense it is). At the start of the brew your wort contains lots of sugars that increase the density of the liquid. This gives you the original gravity (OG) of the beer. As the sugar is turned into alcohol the density decreases. The reading at the end of the fermentation is known as the final gravity (FG). This is very useful information for the following three reasons:

1. You can calculate the alcohol content of the beer. For Alcohol by Volume (ABV) take your OG and subtract your FG then multiply by 131. An example would be OG 1.048 minus FG 1.010 equals 0.038 multiplied by 131 gives 4.97 percent. A useful calculator can be found at: www.brewersfriend.com/abv-calculator

2. A hydrometer can aid judging when a beer is ready to bottle. When the airlock stops bubbling and the foam has disappeared from the surface of the brew then take a hydrometer reading and record it. Wait 2 days and take another reading. If the two readings are the same then fermentation has finished. If the second reading is lower then wait another 2 days and take another reading. Once you have two consecutive readings the same, separated by 2 days, then you can be fairly sure the beer has finished fermenting. The final gravity should be below 1.010 for the majority of beers. There is no need to rush the bottling process—an extra couple of days will benefit the beer by giving it a chance to clear and condition up—but don't leave it more than 3 to 4 days.

3. A hydrometer can help confirm whether or not fermentation has stalled, i.e the yeast has stopped working before 2 to 3 days, the airlock stops bubbling, and the brew stops foaming. It is possible that either fermentation has completed ahead of time or that it has stalled. Give the brew a couple of days, and if the reading is 1.020 or over then fermentation has stalled and you need to take remedial action.

Although a useful tool, it is important that you should not get too obsessed with taking hydrometer readings. It is only necessary at the start of brewing and when you think it has finished. Remember that each time you open the fermenter, you are risking infection from airborne microbes.

Check the gravity when you add the yeast, then leave it alone until the bubbling in the airlock ceases. Checking the gravity in between will not change anything except to possibly risk contamination.

Always remove a sample of the wort to test it. Don't put the hydrometer into the fermetation vessel. Use a sanitized siphon or beer/wine thief to draw a sample of the wort to a hydrometer jar (tall, narrow jar) and float the hydrometer in that. Lower the hydrometer into the jar slowly, since a lot of hydrometers have been broken just hitting the bottom of the jar. Once the hydrometer is in the jar, hold the top between your thumb and finger and gently spin it in the jar to remove bubbles that are clinging to the side of the hydrometer. Take the reading after the hydrometer has stopped spinning.

When reading the hydrometer, put your eye at the level of the liquid and read the number at the bottom of the meniscus (the meniscus is the curvature of the liquid that it makes with the sides of the hydrometer).

Don't put the wort you have tested back into the fermentation bucket (you can drink that to see how it's coming on).

The specific gravity of a liquid is affected by its temperature and most hydrometers are callibrated to read true at 60°F (15°C) Ideally, the liquid should be at 60°F (15°C) when the reading is made, but don't worry, your hydrometer should come with a conversion chart to adjust for higher and lower temperatures. As a guide, 0.001 should be subtracted from the reading for each 9°F (5°C) below 60°F (15°C), and 0.001 added for each 9°F (5°C) above 60°F (15°C).

It is best not to assume that your hydrometer is accurate and you should test it to make sure. Fill your hydrometer flask with water (ideally distilled), which needs to be 60°F (15°C), and dunk the hydrometer. If it reads 1.000 then it is accurate. If not, then take note of the amount that it is out by, as you will need to adjust each reading you take by the same amount.

Thermometer

The thermometer can be a useful tool during the entire process because temperature is an important factor affecting fermentation.

INGREDIENTS

In Bavaria in the 15th century, the world's first regulation concerning the purity of a beverage was made law. This ruling was know as the purity order or *Reinheitsgebot*. It made it known that any unscrupulous brewer who used cheaper ingredients to bulk out their beer and maximize their profits at the expense of quality would be fined and the beer destroyed. Only pure and essential ingredients were to be used in beer, these ingredients being barley, hops and water. Yeast is, of course, an essential ingredient of beer, but it was not known at this time.

In the 1500s, brewers utilized naturally occurring, airborne yeast or took some sediment from the previous fermentation and added it to the next. It is largely because of this that German beer became world renowned for its quality and consistency. German breweries still adhere to the purity law today although it has been reworded to allow yeast.

There is certainly a lot to be said for a law that protects the consumer from being cheated by unscrupulous brewers and, while in Germany cheap ingredients cannot be used simply to bulk out a beer, there is a downside to the *Reinheitsgebot*. The disadvantage is lack of diversity; although there are hundreds of brewers in Germany, most of the beers are very similar. The range of styles of beers brewed by the Germans is not as varied as that of Belgium or the United Kingdom.

Ingredients other than barley, hops, water and yeast are known as adjuncts and they can be used to enhance and add to a beer's qualities rather than just cut down on cost.

It is useful to know why various ingredients are used for brewing beer.

WATER

If your water is pure H_2O it is unsuitable for brewing. All naturally-available water has some mineral content in it and often the best beers are made with water with a high mineral content. Minerals and trace elements have an important role as yeast nutrients and enzyme cofactors.

One reason beer styles vary from region to region is that brewers learned that a beer formulation might produce favorable results in one city, but not in another. Thus beer styles evolved to suit the water of the city in which they were brewed. The water from Burton-on-Trent, with a high sulfite content, contributed to the sharp, clean bitterness of classic pale ale and India pale ale. In Pilsen the very soft water allows the pale color and clean bitterness of Pilsner lager. The water in Munich has a high carbonate content and this leads to low hopping rates and a darker color as found in Dunkel and Bock. In Dublin, water with an extremely high carbonate content required the use of acidic dark malts to achieve a more neutral pH and this led to the classic Dublin stouts.

Chlorine may give a bitter chemical taint to your homebrew. If you fear your tap water is over-chlorinated, you can treat 5 gallons of water with half a Campden tablet.

BARLEY MALT

The barley content of beers comes in many forms. The home brewer can obtain it as grain, crushed grain or malt extract.

Malting is the controlled germination of a cereal, followed by a termination of this process by the application of heat. The malting process produces the enzymatic (diastatic) power to convert starches into fermentable sugars and makes the seed's resources available to the brewer. As well as the sugars that yeast converts to alcohol, the malt also provides more complex, unfermentable carbohydrates that give residual sweetness and body. Proteins in the malt are needed for yeast vitality and head retention. The kilning or roasting of malts yields flavor compounds and adds to the character of beer.

Malts can be classed as either base or speciality malts. Base malts usually account for a large percentage of the total grain content. The proportions of speciality malts in a grist are usually small due to the strength of their flavor and/or color. The commonly used malts include:

Pale ale malt
Pale ale malt provides the bulk of the fermentable sugars in most British beer styles. Pale malt is produced from Maris Otter, Halcyon and Pipkin barley and each variety has its own individual flavor.

Mild ale malt
Mild ale malt is made from barley roasted at a slightly higher temperature than pale ale malt, which results in a darker malt that will give a fuller-flavored beer.

Pilsner malt
Also known as lager malt in the UK, Pilsner malt is the most gently processed base malt that is used in nearly all lagers.

Vienna malt
A base malt that has little color and character but this malt can add a very special, subtle, bread-like aroma to the beer.

Munich malt
A dark base malt, primarily used in the dark Munich style lagers, it can provide a malty aroma to a beer.

Amber malt
Produced by lightly roasting mild ale or chocolate malt, which reduces the harsh flavors of darker roasted grains. Amber malt is used in amber, dark, old and nut brown ales. It is recommended that amber malt should consist of less than 15 percent of the mash and when used well it can provide a

rounded flavor without having too much effect on the color or sweetness of a beer.

Crystal malt

Crystal malt is the most widely used colored malt in the UK and is a standard constituent of a typical ale grist. It is primarily known for its color control, offering adjustments to the depth of the golden red hue during mashing. However, it is also of value for its flavor contribution offering flavors that are nutty, malty, biscuity and those that taste of caramel or toffee. Crystal malt contains a high amount of non-fermentable sugars, and this can provide an amount of body in a beer. The starch in crystal malt has already been converted to sugars, and so does not need to be mashed, it can just as easily be added to the boil, though it is usually put in the mash tun with the rest of the grist.

Brown malt

Brown malt is traditionally used in dark ales, and is kilned over a hardwood fire, imparting a smoky, nutty, caramel flavor. Used in some bitters, mild ales, bocks, porters and stouts.

Chocolate malt

This malt has a smooth, dark roasted flavor with a mocha nuance, and its chocolate color lends its use in dark ales, such as mild ales, stouts, porters and some dark lagers. It can be overpowering when used at a rate of more than 10 percent of the grist.

Black malt

Roasted to a darker color than chocolate malt, black malt's primary use is for its coloring value. It is historically the key ingredient in porter and is also used in other dark beers and stouts. It imparts an astringent, smoky flavor that, although harsh, is less acrid than roasted barley. The sharper, burnt acidic flavor can be inappropiate for dark lagers.

CaraMalt

CaraMalt is a crystal malt with very low color but with a greater degree of sweetness and a stronger caramel flavor. The harsher nutty roasted flavors of crystal malt are not present. It is commonly used in light beers and especially low alcohol lagers because it enhances flavor and character and greatly improves body, foam retention and beer stability while adding little color.

Malt extract

This is a concentrated brewer's wort. It can come as a syrup (liquid malt extract) or a fine, dry granular form sometimes called spray malt or dry malt extract. Extract ranges from extra light to dark with several shades in between, the differing qualities obtained by varying the malts included in the ingredients.

HOPS

Hops (*Humulus lupulus*) are a distant relative of stinging nettle and cannabis. Hops are used for their natural preservative qualities as well as flavoring. The tannins from hops contribute to the bitterness of beer and are also thought to aid in the removal of unwanted proteins during coppering and cooling.

Some hops are added to beer as bittering hops, some as flavoring hops, some as aroma or finishing hops. It is important to know the reasons for adding hops because these qualities require the hops to be added at different stages of the brew. Many beer recipes call for adding hops in two or three stages.

The hops' bitterness comes from alpha acid. The hops intended to bitter a beer are added early during the boil so the heat has time to break down the acid. Hops need to be boiled for around 45 minutes to allow their bittering qualities to penetrate the beer. As the aromatic oils present in hops used to flavor beer are highly volatile, they are easily lost in an extended boil. To capture the flavoring or aroma of hops, brewers add them toward the end of the boil. If boiled for 10 to 20 minutes, the flavor

compounds are released into the beer without adding too much bitterness, but much of the aroma is lost. To capture the delicate hop aroma more hops are added in the last five minutes of the boil.

Adding hops after the boil, usually during the secondary fermentaion stage, is known as dry hopping and is mainly done to add to the aroma but also the taste.

Popular English varieties of hop include:

Bramling Cross
Bramling Cross is a traditional aroma hop making a comeback in cask conditioned beers because of its characteristics. It can be used in many styles of beer.

Challenger
An excellent all-round hop with good bittering and aroma properties. As the main hop it provides a refreshing, full-bodied, rounded bitterness. As the flavoring hop it can give a very crisp, fruity character with spicy overtones, which has proved very popular in many beers.

Fuggle
Probably the most widely known traditional English variety, the Fuggle was the most commonly used aroma hop in England. The development of high alpha varieties have made it less economical for bittering purposes for commercial brewers.

Goldings

A group of traditional English, aroma hop varieties valued for their smooth, delicate, slightly spicy aroma. Like Fuggles, Golding varieties are included in many well-known and respected beers.

Northdown

A general-purpose hop that has been around since the early 1970s. Good bittering properties, while retaining a good, mild flavor. Very popular used either on its own or in conjunction with an aroma variety.

Omega

A bittering hop introduced in the 1980s.

Progress

An aroma hop, introduced by Wye College, Kent, in the 1950s. It is similar to the Fuggle, but a little sweeter with a slightly softer bitterness.

Popular American and European hops:

Cascade

An American cross of Fuggle and a Russian hop, Cascade is a very popular aroma hop with a distinct character. Can be used in almost any American-style beer for bittering as well as aroma.

Hallertauer Hops

The Hallertau district in Bavaria is the largest area of hop production in Europe. The Hallertau produces two main types of hops: Hersbrücker and Northern Brewer. The Hersbrücker is often called Hallertau, but really these hops should be distinguished. There is a variety properly called Hallertau, which formed the stock of the American Hallertau hop. Hallertau Northern Brewer hops are seedless and provide excellent flavor and also very high preservative qualities. Hallertauer Hersbrücker is an aroma hop used in pale German lagers and Pilsners. It can be used in any beer producing a mild, pleasant hop aroma.

Northern Brewer

Northern Brewer, when produced in the United States, has strong woody or minty qualities. Very good for bittering porters, stouts, or American steam beers. The German version has slightly better aromatic qualities. Derived from Northern Brewer, Northdown hops are grown in England and share many of the same characteristics, and have replaced Northern Brewer in much of the UK for all uses, including dry Irish stouts. A clean and mild bitterness with a delicate hop aroma.

Saaz

Possibly the best aroma hop, the Czech Saaz is the original Pilsner hop. Saaz is the only choice when brewing Pilsners. It is excellent in all European-style lagers for bittering and flavor. It can be scarce and expensive.

Styrian Goldings

An aroma hop with widespread usage in both ale and lager brewing. Not really a Golding and is more akin to the Fuggle hop.

YEAST

The main distinction between different types of beer comes from the two types of yeast used in their production. The top fermenting yeast, *Saccharomyces cerevisiae* produces a light frothy 'head' on the beer and is used to produce ales, including bitters, porters and stout.

The bottom fermenting yeast, *Saccharomyces carlsbergenis*, is used to produce lager, which tends to be crisper and cooler than bitter and retains more carbonation. It is vital to pamper the yeast while it is working by ensuring that the brew is at the correct temperature. This is because the yeast's by-products, as it converts sugar to alcohol, supply most of the beer's flavor. If the yeast is too hot, too many flavor compounds are produced, if too cold, the beer can taste pretty bland. Generally speaking, ale yeasts like warmer temperatures, 64°F (18°C) or so, while lager yeasts will happily work at 50°F (10°C). (Lager yeast can be used at ale temperatures to produce California common beer.) It is most important to keep the temperature of your fermenting wort steady. A sharp fluctuation in temperature is likely to stop your yeast from working.

Within the two types of yeasts, various strains have been developed. Different yeast strains will produce different beers when pitched to identical worts.

Yeast is available both wet and dry. For the first-time brewer, a dry ale yeast is highly recommended. Liquid yeasts are on the whole considered to be superior to dry yeasts. The strain of liquid yeast you use is a crucial determinant with regard to the finished beer's flavor. Liquid yeast adds its own unique flavor to the brew but liquid yeasts can be five times as expensive as dried yeasts. Hence, dried yeasts end up being more commonly used.

Yeast starter

The quality of your homebrew can be dramatically improved by making a yeast starter. You can sprinkle a packet of yeast into your wort and the fermentation will mostly be successful, but creating a yeast starter will promote complete fermentation, reduce the risk of infection and improve the overall quality of your beer. A starter can be made by dissolving dry malt extract, boiling it for 10 to 15 minutes to make sure it is sterile, and then cooling it quickly in an ice bath. Transfer it to a sanitized container. Once it reaches room temperature, pitch your yeast and seal the container with an airlock to prevent contamination. After about 24 hours pitch the entire contents of the starter into your batch of beer to get an active, robust start.

ADJUNCTS

The definition of adjunct varies between

brewers. To many, adjuncts are only unmalted grains such as corn, rice, rye, oats, barley and wheat. Under the Bavarian purity law, any ingredient other than water, barley, yeast and hops is considered an adjunct. This is a bit pedantic, but for convenience's sake we shall use this meaning.

Flaked corn

Known as maize in the UK, corn is a popular adjunct with many brewers. Flaked corn can add fullness to a beer. It should not be used in proportions of over 15 percent of total ingredients or the flavor can become obtrusive.

Flaked rice

Flaked rice is used as an alternative to flaked corn. Some brewers prefer rice because of its lower oil content compared to corn. Rice has hardly any taste of its own, which is regarded as a positive characteristic since rice will not interfere with the basic malt character of the beer.

Barley

Unmalted barley gives a rich, smooth, grainy flavor to beer and will contribute head retention to the finished beer. The use of torrified (subjected to intense heat) barley can give a nutty/chewy mouthfeel.

Roast barley

This is simply raw barley that has been roasted to a dark reddish brown color. Its dry, slightly bitter burnt flavor is the defining taste of Irish type stouts. It can be used sparingly to darken other beers. Not as rich in flavor as black malt.

Wheat

Unmalted wheat is used to enhance body, head retention and foam stability. Care should be taken when using wheat as flour as it can "dough" and cause the other contents of a mash to glue together resulting in set mashes.

Oats

Flaked oats can be used to give a smooth, creamy finish, particularly in brewing oatmeal stout. The high oil content can have adverse effects on the head retention of a beer.

Sugar

Too high a level of sugar, or a mash with a high level of maltose, will produce a thin beer, but there are many types of sugar that

can be used in moderation, to add various qualities to a beer.

Dextrose or glucose can be added to produce body and impart a nutty flavor.

Partially refined cane sugars such as demerara can be used in ales and leave a mellow, sweet flavor. Darker sugars like barbados and muscovado contribute stronger flavor due to the higher content of molasses.

Invert sugar is used to increase alcohol in some Belgian or English ales and can be used as a priming sugar. When used in Belgian beers the liquid invert sugar is known as candy sugar. The Belgian strong ales can have an ABV of as much as 10 percent, but these beers are still very easy drinking. This is because they are as light in body as a normal beer, due to the use of Belgian candy sugar. This adds alcohol but, the candy sugar has been caramelized, and this gives nice complex flavors.

Lactose adds sweetness and body and is used in sweet or milk stouts.

Golden syrup comprises 50 percent liquid invert sugar and is used by many English brewers. It boosts gravity without altering flavor. Add during boil for authentic bitters, milds and other English ales.

Caramel is used mainly as a coloring agent.

Since the early days of brewing, honey was often used in beer when other forms of sugar were not easily available. It can produce inconsistent results and is now more expensive than other sugars.

Herbs

Hops are by far the most common herb used by brewers but this has not always been the case. Hops have been in common use in European beers since the 1400s. Prior to this, beer often contained herbs such as bog myrtle, rosemary, yarrow, alecost and many others. The herbs were not only chosen for their bitterness, flavor or aromatic qualities but also for their reputed medicinal properties. Many commercial brewers as well as home brewers are reassessing these herbs and their use in modern beers.

The use of an herb depends on the qualities of the herb and the kind of beer you wish to brew. Some herbs have many useful qualities but none are as versatile as hops. Even when using other herbs it is usual to include some hops in the recipe.

Sage, dandelion, alecost, nettle and yarrow can be used for bittering. They are added at the beginning of the boil in place of, or in addition to, bittering hops.

Herbs that can be used for flavoring include ginger, sweet woodruff, juniper and liquorice. These herbs are usually added near the beginning of the boil.

Lavender, chamomile, elderflowers and many other herbs can be used to provide aroma to beer. Any aromatic herb can be used for dry hopping or added in the last few minutes of the boil.

Fruit

Perhaps the most distinctive of all Belgian brews are the fruit beers. Kriek is flavoured by cherries and Framboise by raspberries. The practice of using fruit to flavor beers is now being taken up by brewers in Britain, America and other parts of the world. Other fruits that are used to flavor beer include apple, blackberry, cranberry, kiwi, rhubarb and lemon.

When using fresh fruit, add it to the beer after the primary fermentation. The beer needs to have an ABV of at least 5 percent, because you need this alcohol to kill off any microorganisms that may be present on the fruit.

BEER STYLES

All beers can be classified into either lager types or ales by the yeast used to brew them and the temperature at which they are brewed. Lager uses yeast that ferments at the bottom of the brewing vessel and works best at cooler temperatures. Beer classified as ale uses another type of yeast that ferments on the top of the vessel and works best at warmer temperatures. Ales come in a variety of colors from dark golden to deep brown or black. Likewise, the strength of flavor of an ale can vary between a very delicate palate to a heavily hopped, extremely assertive flavor. Although there are generally only two types of beer, both lager and ale can be further sub-divided in to many styles that have evolved over centuries of brewing.

LAGERS

Pilsner

Pilsner originated in Czechoslovakia in the 1840s and is today the world's most popular style of beer. Pilsners are very light in color, malty sweet, and well-hopped with a medium to high bitterness. They have a good amount of carbonation and are clean and crisp.

Pale lager

Pale lager is the standard international style of lager that derives ultimately from Pilsner, but is characterized by a lighter color and much less body and taste. American lagers achieve a low gravity by adding corn or rice syrup, which are highly fermentable. This results in a higher percentage of sugars turning into alcohol leaving behind less flavor. Pale lagers are often dismissed as being bland and watery but despite this, they sell well and consequently must appeal to many people.

Bock

The origin of Bock beer is a bit uncertain, although it is thought it was first brewed in Munich in the early 1600s, with the aid the skills of a brewer from Einbeck. The use of Munich malt as the primary grain for a Bock recipe is the main factor in this beer's character, as it provides a unique flavor and color contribution to the beer. The higher gravities required for a Bock can stretch the limits of a home brewer's mash capacities, but luckily an excellent Bock can be made using a small mash backed up with a large amount of malt extract. Bock beers require little or no hop flavor or aroma and have low levels of bitterness. Bock beers typically have an ABV of 5 to 6 percent.

Doppelbocks, as the name suggests, are extra strong, rich and weighty, and typically 7 to 8 percent ABV. The intense malty sweetness of Doppelbock is balanced with a note of hop bitterness.

Dunkel

Dunkel means "dark," so the term can be applied to any dark beer, even to dark top-fermented wheat beer, but it generally refers to a style of dark lager that originated in Bavaria. All lagers were dark until breweries in Pilsen started brewing golden lagers in the 1840s. From the 1890s onward, dark lagers gradually gave way to the paler lagers.

Dark lagers are brewed with a darker roasted malt than pale lagers and have a distinctive taste. Dunkel lagers should combine the dry chocolate or licorice notes associated with the use of dark roasted malts and the roundness and crisp character of a lager.

Vienna-style lager

This reddish-amber lager with a very malty toasted character and a hint of sweetness was originally brewed in Austria in the 10th century, and has come to be known as the Vienna style. The style was adapted by the Munich brewers and in their hands has a noted malty sweetness and toasted flavor with a touch more richness.

Eisbock

This is lager that is frozen after brewing and then has some of the ice removed. This process removes water, leaving you with a more concentrated beer, both in terms of flavor and alcoholic strength, which can be 15 percent!

BEERS

Although mainly associated with the traditional beer styles of Britain and Belgium, top fermented beers are produced throughout the world. Among them:

Bitter and pale ales

Originally pale ale was beer made from malt, kilned over coke, a fuel made by heating coal to remove the gas and tar. The resulting solid substance burns hot and steady and the resulting malt produced was a clear, amber-colored ale that was far paler than any British ales brewed before the availability of pale malt. Bitter is essentially an offshoot of the style of beer traditionally known as pale ale. Bitter initially referred to pale ales that had a noticeably higher hop content. Although once considered a sub-style of pale ale, the term bitter has now more or less replaced that of pale ale. For many brewers, pale ale is their name for a bottled version of a bitter.

Bitter is the mainstay of a good British pub and is best enjoyed when cask-conditioned in the pub's cellar and dispensed through a hand-pump. India pale ales were brewed to be strong in alcohol and high in hops. The preservative qualities of the hops and alcohol helped to keep the beers in good condition during long sea journeys.

Bitter can range from 3 to 7 percent ABV. Bitters with less than 4 percent are classed as session bitters. Most India pale ales from Britian fall into this group. Mid-range strength bitters up to 4.7 percent ABV are often called best bitter. Stronger bitters are known as premium or extra special bitter (in the United States, especially).

Mild

Mild ale is a lighter bodied, but usually darker colored, beer with a relatively low hop content and an ABV content typically around 3.5 percent. In the 1940s, mild was more popular than bitter in British pubs, though now it can be hard to find.

Porter

Porters are dark and full-bodied beers. Porters usually have a more noticeable barley flavor, which is reminiscent of chocolate, along with a mild hop flavor.

Porter is said to have gained its name through its popularity with the transportation workers of London in the early 19th century—when the city was still a thriving commercial port. At this time it was a popular practice to mix two or three beers, usually an old, or stale, brown ale with a new brown ale and a pale ale. Eventually a brewer produced a new beer, known as "entire," to match the tastes of such mixtures. Using high roasted malts, entire was dark, cloudy and hoppy. It was also easily produced in bulk and ideally suited to the soft well-water of London. Particularly strong types of porter came to be referred to as stout porter, from the usage of stout to mean "strong" or "robust."

Stout

Stouts are the darkest type of beer, being almost black in color. They are thick and taste strongly of the barley and hops that they are made from. Stout is brewed from roasted grains, giving it the characteristic opaque black hue. There are various styles of stout, the well-hopped dry stouts, milk stouts, which contain lactose, and also oatmeal, chocolate and coffee stouts.

Brown ale

Quite a recent beer, first created in the early 1900s, brown ale is a lighter, less hoppy version of a classic dark ale. Reddish-brown in color, it is relatively low in alcohol but also quite rounded and full in flavor.

Barley wine

Barley wines are extremely potent ales that can range from golden copper to dark brown in color. They date from the 18th and 19th centuries, a period when England was often at war with France and an alternative to French wine was required. They are characterized by strong caramel malt flavors and bittering hops that prevent the rich, malt sweetness from being cloying. Many barley wines are vintage dated and improve with age. The sweetness and strength make them highly suitable to be consumed after dinner or with dessert. Barley wines are usually fermented with an ale yeast, creating a signature fruity aroma. However, some brewers use a high-alcohol tolerant yeast more suited to champagne or wine fermentation, to ensure a complete attenuation.

Red, golden and amber ales

These are American, modern styles of beer that borrow heavily from more classical, British styles such as pale ale or bitter. Generally speaking they will have less body, hop and malt character than a pale ale.

Altbier

As lager brewing spread from Bohemia, some German brewers retained the top fermenting ale process but adopted the cold maturation associated with lager. Hence the name "Old Beer" (*alt* means old in German). This style of ale is light to medium-bodied, less fruity, less yeasty and has lower acidity than a traditional British ale.

Abbey ales

These abbey ales can vary enormously in character, but are usually quite strong in alcoholic content ranging between 6 and 10 percent ABV. Abbey ales are often referred to as either Singel, Dubbel or Tripel to denote the alcoholic content. Singels and dubbels are often darker beers, while the tripels are often blond in color and have a syrupy, alcoholic mouthfeel that invites sipping, not quaffing.

Bière de Garde

Bière de Garde was traditionally brewed in northern French and Flemish farmhouses in early spring, bottled in champagne bottles, corked and left to age. It is brewed to be kept until the summer months when the warmer weather doesn't permit brewing. *Bière de garde* literally means "keeping beer." It is a strong, yet refreshing and delicate bottle-conditioned beer, and tends to be profoundly aromatic. It is an excellent accompaniment to hearty foods.

Wheat beer

There are quite a few sub-styles of wheat beer. Typically wheat beers contain between 30 and 70 percent wheat malt and the remainder is usually a pale barley malt. The various wheat beers all share certain traits. The wheat does not contribute a lot of flavor and wheat beers often contain a bit of flavoring from adjuncts like fruit and spices. The higher protein content of wheat contributes to thick, long-lasting heads. This protein also causes the haze in most wheat beers. The light, effervescent nature of wheat beers makes them an ideal drink for a hot summer's day.

BREWING FROM A KIT

THE HOMEBREW KIT

Most novices start off by brewing from a kit. It is a good way to start, with many advantages over brewing full or partial mashes as it is cheaper, a whole lot simpler, quicker and takes up less space.

Some people, however, try brewing from kits and give up after one or two attempts, less than happy with the results. There is no reason why you should fail to brew a good, drinkable beer, it is just a matter of following the instructions. Hopefully by following a few extra directions it will increase your chances of success.

Firstly, choose the style of beer you wish to brew. Just about every style of beer is now available as a kit. To increase your chances of success, bear in mind it is easier to brew a bottom-fermented ale than it is a lager. Also, an average strength brew of around 4 to 5 percent ABV would be a better choice than, say, a barley wine.

Some kits are made from just concentrated, hopped wort and others have half the fermentable material supplied by adding cane sugar. Although both are just as likely to ferment successfully given the same conditions, the beer made with sugar is unlikely to taste quite as good as one made using a100 percent concentrate kit.

The following list of instructions are similar to those that come with an average homebrew bitter kit.

1. Clean all equipment with sanitizing solution.

2. Remove the label and stand the can in hot water for 5 minutes to soften contents.

3. While the contents are softening, boil 4 quarts (3.5 liters) of water.

4. Open the can and pour the contents into your cleaned and sterilized fermentation container (minimum 26 quarts, 25 liters).

5. Add the boiling water to the fermentation container.

6. Add 2 pounds (1 kilogram) of sugar.

7. Mix the contents thoroughly to dissolve the sugar and malt extract.

8. Add 20 quarts (19 liters) of cold water to bring the volume up to about 24 quarts (23 liters). Stir and leave to stand until the temperature reaches 64 to 70°F (18 to 21°C).

9. Sprinkle the yeast supplied onto the liquid and stir.

10. Cover the fermenting container with the lid and place in a warm area.

11. Now leave to ferment.

12. Fermentation will be complete when bubbles have stopped rising (between 4 to 6 days).

13. Siphon the bitter into either a pressurized container or bitter bottles.

14. Add half a heaping teaspoon of sugar per 20 fl oz (591 ml) to each bottle.

15. Cap and seal the bottles and stand in a warm place for 2 days.

16. Move the bottles or barrel to a cool place for 14 days or until the bitter is clear before drinking.

There is nothing wrong with following the instructions on the can, but it can be improved upon. Follow steps 1 and 2 as per instructions and then:

• Boil approximately 7 fl oz (200 ml) of water and cool. When the water is below 86°F (30°C), stir in the yeast. Cover, wait 10 minutes then stir in 1 heaping teaspoon of sugar. Cover and place in a warm area out of direct sunlight.

• While the yeast is hydrating, heat 5 to 11 quarts (5 to 10 liters) of water to boiling point, add to the fermentation bucket, then add the contents of the can of wort concentrate and sugar if your kit requires

it. Dissolve well and add enough cold (preferably pre-boiled) water to bring to the final volume.

• Cover and allow to cool to room temperature. Pre-boiling the water used to top up will remove chlorines and kill any bacteria present.

• When the wort is at room temperature (81°F, 27°C, or below), and not before, add the yeast and stir. Cover well, making sure that no air can get in, but that the carbon dioxide generated by the yeast can get out.

• Keep at room temperature (63 to 72°F, 17 to 22°C) for several days. Fermentation should start within 12 hours, and it should start to subside in 3 to 4 days. Leave the beer in the fermenter for 5 to 7 days after the fermentation has subsided.

• Clean, sanitize and rinse all equipment that will contact the beer during bottling.

• Use 4.5 oz to 5 oz (130 g to 150 g) of cane sugar to prime 20 quarts (19 liters) of beer, or 5 oz to 6 oz (150 g to 170 g) to prime 24 quarts (23 liters). Do not overprime—it is better to have under-carbonated beer than to have exploding bottles. Boil 2 quarts (2 liters) of water, add the sugar, stir and let it simmer for 5 minutes. This is your priming solution. Pour it into a sanitized priming bucket, cover and cool to room temperature.

- Place your fermenting bucket on a counter top or table and your priming bucket on the floor below. Attach your siphon tubing to the sediment trap. Make sure you have enough tubing to reach from the sediment trap in the bucket to the bottom of the priming bucket. Siphon the beer off the sediment, being careful not to splash the beer. Avoid aeration in this step. You should not need to stir the beer if you have put the priming solution in the priming bucket before the beer.

- The beer can now be transferred to bottles. Leave a 2- in (5-cm) gap between the top of the liquid and the bottle cap, but don't crimp the caps straight away. Leave them with caps in place but uncrimped for half an hour. This allows the beer to produce some CO_2, which will drive out some of the air in the bottles. Now crimp the caps.

- Keep bottles in a warm place for 2 days and then store in a cool place for at least 14 days.

There are three main things to remember when brewing beer, or in fact any type of beverage—PREPARATION, SANITATION and KEEPING RECORDS. This applies to brewing from a kit, too. Good preparation means that you will never get caught out; you wouldn't want to get halfway through your brewing before realizing that you don't actually have any yeast. You also wouldn't want to pour a good wort into a fermenter that you had forgotten to clean properly. Cleaning and sanitizing are both part of your preparation, and are essential factors for ensuring a successful batch of beer. In fact, it would be fair to say that good brewing is 75 percent cleaning!

Be consistent, and you should produce an above-average brew. This is where good record keeping comes in. Always keep good notes on what ingredients you used, how long it took to ferment and whether you needed to add any extra ingredients, etc. There are several brewing spreadsheets and software programs that are available over the internet that can be really helpful.

Keeping thorough records is the only way that a brewer will be able to repeat a good batch and learn from poor ones. It is no good just leaving it to memory, because however good your memory is, you can guarantee you won't remember everything.

These are the main headings you should use in your records, and make sure you understand any abbreviations you use:

- Recipe title
- Volume made
- Yeast
- Malt
- Hops
- Sugar
- Procedure
- Fermentation
- Results

MALT EXTRACT BREWS

With homebrew kits you are in effect brewing with a pre-made hopped wort. The grains have not only been chosen, malted and mashed for you, but the hops have been added too. There is another way of brewing that is still uncomplicated but gives you just a little more control over the finished beer.

When brewing with malt extracts it is more like brewing with a pre-made sweet wort to which you add the hops' qualities. You will need a bit more equipment than you do when brewing from a kit but not nearly so much as when brewing a full mash. You will need something to strain the hops from the wort. A nylon mesh, sparge bag would be ideal or failing that some muslin cloth. A large boiler or saucepan is also needed, something with a capacity of at least 16 quarts (15 liters).

Here for example is a recipe and simple, basic method to brew a stout:

MALT EXTRACT STOUT

Ingredients
2 lb (900 g) pale malt extract
1 lb (450 g) dark malt extract
1.5 oz (40 g) Goldings hops

Method
1. Put 3 quarts (3 liters) of hot water into your pot, add all of the extract and stir well to dissolve. Top up the water to 11 quarts (10 liters) and bring to the boil. Just as the solution boils add 75 percent of the hops. Boil for 50 minutes, add the remainder of the hops and boil for a further 10 minutes.

2. Transfer the wort to the fermenting bucket, straining the hops out. Top up the wort with boiling water to 13 quarts or 12 liters (the extra water allows for some loss during raking). Speed up the cooling of the

wort by standing the pot in cool water, swirl the cool water around the outside of the pot occasionally. When the wort is around 70°F (21°C) take a hydrometer reading (adjust reading for temperature), adjust the density as required by adding water or sugar and then pitch the yeast.

3. Fit the lid and airlock to the bucket and put it in a warm place, out of direct sunlight. The active fermentation should take 3 to 4 days, leave it another 5 to 7 days and take another gravity reading to ensure fermentation is complete and also to work out the alcohol content.

4. Bottle in the same way as described earlier for the homebrew kit. You will need 2 to 3 ounces (65 to 75 grams) of cane sugar to prime the 11 quarts (10 liters) of beer produced.

You can use this same method with different ingredients to produce other styles of beers, for example:

BROWN ALE
Ingredients
2 lb (900 g) pale dried malt extract
0.5 lb (225 g) medium-dark dried malt
   extract
0.5 lb (225 g) dark dried malt extract
1 oz (30 g) Goldings hops
For brown ale follow the method for stout but all of the hops should be added at the beginning of the boil. Boil for 60 minutes.

MILD ALE
Ingredients
2 lb (900 g) pale dried malt extract
1 lb (450 g) dark malt extract
1.5 oz (40 g) Fuggles hops

Like brown ale, add all of the hops at the start of the boil. Boil for 60 minutes.

PALE ALE
Ingredients
3 lb (1.25 kg) pale dried malt extract
3.5 oz (100 g) medium-dark dried malt
   extract
1.5 oz (40 g) Goldings hops

As with stout, add 75 percent of the hops at start of boil and the rest 10 minutes before the end of the boil.

BREWING PARTIAL AND FULL MASHES

THE FULL MASH

Whether you use grains or not, knowing a little about the mashing process will help you understand more about brewing.

Malting

Beer is brewed from malted barley. Malting is the process where the barley seed is soaked in water and then allowed to germinate. After the barley has germinated it is dried and kilned. How long the barley is allowed to germinate, and the time and temperature of kilning can be varied to produce different types of malts for different brewing purposes. Pale malts are typically kilned in the range of 158° to 176°F (70° to 80°C), darker malts such as Munich and Vienna are kilned in the range of 194° to 230°F (90° to 110°C).

During germination, the seeds produce enzymes that will help them draw on their energy reserves so they can grow into plants. During the mashing process, these enzymes react with the starches in the malt and produce maltose. Maltose is a favorite food for yeast during fermentation.

Mashing

Mashing is a step in the brewing process when crushed malts are steeped in hot water in a mash tun. Different enzymes do different jobs and are activated at different temperatures. The most important enzymes are the alpha and beta-amylases, which convert malt starches to fermentable malt sugars. Because they work in slightly different ways and at slightly different temperatures, varying the temperature of the mash alters the fermentable qualities of the wort and hence the characteristics of the final beer. They both break up bonds between the glucose molecules in starch.

In all grain-brewing, temperature control is absolutely critical since the amylase activities must be balanced out. Alpha-amylase is most active in the range 149° to 162°F (to 65° to 72°C), for beta-amylase 122° to 149°F (50° to 65°C) is the range at which it is most active. Most mashing temperatures are around 149° to 151°F (65° to 66°C). This is not only a point where both enzymes are active but also the temperature at which the starch gelatinizes. This liquifying of the starch makes it more accessible to both enzymes. One or two degrees does make a difference. Worts mashed at less than 149°F (65°C) need more time because the starch has not been gelatinized, and alpha amylase activity is slow. Worts mashed above 154°F (68°C) can produce beers that are overly sweet and cloying because the beta-amylase starts to break up at the higher temperature.

If beta-amylase activity is allowed to dominate and convert all of the starch into glucose or maltose, the result would be a highly fermentable wort that would produce a very dry, alcoholic beer with very low residual sugar levels. Brewers aim to have some alpha-amylase activity in the mash for non-fermentable sugars that will provide more body and mouthfeel to the beer.

Mashing crushed malts is not easy to achieve without the right equipment. There are a few options available to the home brewer.

A 29-quart (27-liter) boiler complete with a thermostat, heating element and tap would make the process easier. It would enable you to set and automatically maintain an accurate mash temperature throughout the mashing period. A false bottom or sparge bag would prevent the grain accumulating around the heating element.

You could use a large pot on a stove top or burner with a thermometer to monitor the temperature. This could be a good option for a small trial run at a mash with a scaled down recipe.

Another option is using an insulated mash tun. This could be a large picnic cooler fitted with extra insulation and with a slotted manifold inside attached to a tap. The idea is that when the tap is opened the manifold allows the liquid to drain out, but leaves the grain where it is. As there is no heating element in the tun, the water and the tun have to be pre-heated. The tun is pre-heated by pouring a couple of quarts of boiling water into it, closing the lid and giving it a gentle swirl. Leave it for a few

minutes, while you boil another pot of water. Run the water out of the mash tun through the tap and repeat the process with the next pot of water.

After emptying the tun of the second batch of pre-heating water, close the tap and fill it with water heated to 169°F (76°C). Wait for this water to drop to 167°F (75°C) and then add the grain and stir well. Make sure you make a good loose porridge, mixing the grain and water well and breaking up any lumps.

Take the temperature of the mash in several places and get an average. It should be at about 153°F (67°C). If it is over 158°F (70°C) carefully add cold water to bring the temperature down. If it is under 145°F (63°C), you can do the same with hot water from the pot. Once you have the temperature right, fit the lid. The insulated tun should keep the mash at the required temperature for the required duration of the mash.

Starch test

When mashing at 149°F (65°C) all conversion of the starch into sugars should be achieved within an hour. This can be confirmed with an iodine test.

After an hour of mashing, take a little liquid free from grains, and drop it onto a white plate. Add two drops of tincture of iodine to the sample. If the sample turns blue or blue-black, starches are still present; continue mashing and testing until there is no change in the color of the sample. No color change indicates no starches are present and mashing is complete. Discard the sample—use a fresh plate for each test.

Sparging

Sparging is sprinkling hot water over the mash to rinse the fermentable sugars from the grain. The rinsing helps to extract about 70 to 80 percent of the fermentable sugars from the grain. There are two common methods used by home brewers, continuous and batch sparging.

Continuous sparging is a popular method similar to how the big breweries sparge. A sprinkler is positioned over the mash, and water is trickled over the grains to drain the sugars. The amount of sparging water is equal to the amount of water added to the grain. This trickling of water rinses the grains and also uses the grain bed as a filter to keep back any solids.

One way of continuous sparging is to position the mash tun over another vessel large enough to contain the whole of the wort (if your mash used 13 quarts, 12 liters, of water your final wort will be around 25 quarts, 24 liters). Above the mash tun you will need a 16-quart (15-liter) bucket filled with water at 167°F (75°C), with a tap and a hose with a sprinkler/shower head attached to this. Open the tap on the mash tun slowly and collect the first quart or two in a jug. Take this and slowly pour it back into the mash tun so as to not disturb the grain bed. Repeat three or four times or until there is no particulate matter coming out

and the wort is fairly clear. This is called the *vorlauf* and is used to help set the grain bed to be used as a filter when you are draining. After this slowly open the tap on the sparging bucket with the sprinkler head aimed at the grains. You need to adjust both taps so that the sparging water does not disturb or rise above the level of the grain bed and the tap from the mash tun runs as fast as you can sparge. The grains should not be disturbed because they act as a filter, but move the sprinkler head slowly over all of the top of the grain bed to wash out as much sugar as possible.

Strictly speaking, the batch method is not really sparging, since batch sparging removes the sugars from the grain through dilution. The grain is not rinsed through. Using the batch sparging method, your goal is to collect the total wort in two mash tun runnings. The first running will be the wort collected from your initial mash. The second will be the wort collected from your sparge.

When the mash is complete, the wort is drained completely, going through the *vorlauf* process as before. The mash tun is filled with the sparge water. The temperature should be around 167°F (75°C). The grain bed is stirred to get the sugars back into the solution, and then allowed to settle for about 10 minutes. Drain off the sparge water, again returning the *vorlauf*.

There may be a lower efficiency for batch sparging but this reduced efficiency can be allowed for with a 5 to 10 percent higher grain content or an extract addition to your wort. Adding extract at the end is probably the best method because the target gravity is easily achieved and the wort can be adjusted to reach it.

Boiling

After the production of the sweet wort, it is then boiled. There are a number of reasons for this. Most of the hops are added at this stage. As well as accommodating the hops' schedule, the boil also sterilizes the wort, deactivates the enzymes and stabilizes the proteins.

Many recipes require you to add some hops near the beginning of the boil, somewhere in the middle and the rest during the last 5 minutes. Hops are added in these staggered additions because as some qualities of the hops break down during the boil, the more delicate aspects, such as the aroma and flavor, evaporate away. Conversely, the longer they are in the boil, the more of their bittering qualities are released and absorbed into the wort. Therefore the hops that go in early in the boil, will bitter your beer. The hops that go in towards the end of the boil will add to the aroma and flavor.

When it comes from the mash tun, wort contains among other things, a lot of different proteins. An important function of the boil is to remove some of these proteins, which can cause side effects ranging from chill haze to off flavors. It is important to boil the wort for at least 1 hour and to maintain a rolling boil for that whole time

to stabilize the brew. The aim is to remove most of, but not all of, the proteins from a wort because they are responsible for some needed qualities including color and mouthfeel.

Hops play an important role in the process of removing these unwanted proteins. The proteins will stick to the polyphenols from the hops. A vigorous boil assures that these polyphenols will actively move about in the pot and gather as many of the proteins as possible. These unstable proteins gather as little clouds in the brew. These clouds then precipitate to the bottom of the pot at the end of the boil. This is known as the hot break. This is probably the most important aspect of the boil as it removes the potentially harmful proteins.

Cooling

When the wort is hot, bacteria and wild yeasts are inhibited but it is very susceptible to oxidation damage as it cools. At the end of the boil, it is important to cool the wort quickly. Rapid cooling prevents the causes of spoilage before the yeast gets working and protects the beer with a layer of gas above the fermenting wort.

Cooling also brings on the cold break. This causes another group of proteins to be thermally shocked into precipitating out of the wort. Cold break can help prevent the cause of chill haze. Chill haze is usually regarded as a cosmetic problem. You cannot taste it. However, chill haze indicates that there is an appreciable level of protein in the beer, which could affect long-term stability.

The wort can be cooled by placing the pot in a sink or tub filled with cold/ice water that can be circulated around the hot pot. If the cooling water gets warm, replace with colder water. The wort should cool to 81°F (27°C) in about 30 minutes. When the pot is barely warm to the touch, the temperature is in the right range. This method is fine for a small brew of 11 to 16 quarts (10 to 15 liters) but for larger volumes a wort chiller is easier and safer.

A wort chiller is a coil of copper tubing that is used as a heat exchanger. Wort chillers are useful for cooling full volume boils because you don't need to move a boiler full of hot wort to a sink or bathtub.

Immersion wort chillers work by running cold water through the coil, which is immersed in the wort.

Removal of trub

Trub is a collection of material resulting from the cold and hot breaks and also the hops sitting on the bottom of the boiling pot after cooling. This material is best removed before fermentation. Although the hops are harmless, and the cold break relatively so, the hot break material can cause off flavors.

The most common method for separating the wort from the trub is to carefully decant the wort into the fermenter, leaving the trub behind. Pouring the wort through a stainless steel strainer can also help with this approach. If you are siphoning the cooled wort from the pot, whirlpooling can help.

Whirlpooling is a means of gathering most of the trub and hops into the center of the pot to better enable the siphon to draw off clear wort from the side. Rapidly stir the wort in a circular manner. Continue until all the liquid is moving and a whirlpool forms. Stop stirring and let the whirlpool slow down and settle for 10 minutes or so. The whirlpooling action will form a pile in the center of the pot, leaving the edge relatively clear. The siphon won't clog as quickly now if it draws from the side of the pot.

Aeration of wort

Yeast needs oxygen to function. You can aerate the wort by allowing vigorous churning and splashing when pouring or siphoning the wort into the fermentation vessel.

Fermentation

After straining the wort into the fermenting bucket, top up with cold, pre-boiled water to the required volume. When temperature has cooled to 70 to 77°F (21 to 25°C), take a hydrometer reading, adjust as necessary by adding pre-boiled water or sugar, and then add the yeast.

Place the fermenter in a warm area that is not exposed to direct sunlight and has a stable temperature around 64 to 75°F (18 to 24°C). Place the fermenter on a shallow tray or towel to collect any foam that may escape through the airlock.

Active fermentation should start within 24 hours and the airlock bubbling regularly will indicate this. The fermentation activity will slow down after about 3 days. It is at this stage that many brewers rack off the beer in to another vessel for secondary fermentation. This is not necessary for most normal strength ales and causes risk of spoilage through infection, unwanted oxidation and extra work. Better to leave the beer in the original fermenter for 5 to 7 days and let the secondary fermentation carry on in the bottles or barrel.

For lagers and higher alcohol brews it is worthwhile to have a secondary fermenter to transfer to after the initial vigorous primary fermentation has taken place (which, for lagers, may take 10 days). This is to remove the fermenting beer from most of the trub (materials that precipitate from the beer) and therefore prevent undesirable flavors.

THE PARTIAL MASH

A method of brewing also called mini-mash or half mash is partial mashing—a halfway point between extract brewing and all-grain brewing. Strictly speaking, a partial mash is using the enzymes from a diastatic active malt extract to convert starches from other beer adjuncts such as flaked and torrified barleys and flaked wheat. To use the enzymatic reaction, the wort is kept at 151°F (66°C) for 30 to 45 minutes in the boiler before slowly raising the temperature to 167°F (75°C) to stall the reaction. The wort is then boiled as usual.

Many home brewers also use the term to describe recipes using a small amount of mashed grains combined with malt extract.

It is also sometimes used for the practice of steeping grains in extract brewing.

For the purpose of this book, we shall use the looser definition of a partial mash being a combination of a small amount of grains with a large part of the fermentable sugars provided by malt extract.

MUNICH HELLES LAGER

Here is an easy partial mash method that does not require a lot of extra equipment. It will produce about 24 quarts (23 liters) of a moderately hopped and malty lager in the style of a Munich Helles with a specific gravity of about 1.045.

The main equipment needed is:
• Thermometer
• Insulated mashing tun with tap
• Large grain bag
• Large saucepan/stockpot that can hold 16 to 21 quarts (15 to 20 liters)

Ingredients
   3.5 lb (1.5 kg) can of extra pale malt
      extract
   4 lb (2 kg) of Vienna malt
   1.75 oz (50 g) of Hallertau Hersbrucker
      hops
   Lager yeast

Method
1. Bring 15 quarts (14 liters) of water to 153° to 154°F (67° to 68°C), which is slightly above the target mash temperature. Add half of this to the mash tun, stir in the grain

then about 0.5 ounce (20 g) of hops. Stir in the rest of the water, checking the mash temperature as you do. When satisfied with the mash temperature, close the mash tun and leave the mash to convert.

2. After 40 minutes check the mash temperature. If it has fallen more than a few degrees below the ideal of 149° to 151°F (65° to 66°C) then add 1 quart (1 liter) of boiling water. Leave for 20 minutes more; the mash should be fully converted.

3. Slowly run the wort off into the saucepan. Use a tube on the end of the tap so that the wort does not splash and become aerated.

4. Boil the wort for 30 minutes. Add the remaining hops and boil for a further 45 minutes. Add finings as per instructions. The boil should be vigorous and the pot uncovered. When the boil has finished the wort needs to be cooled as quickly as possible. Place the lid on the pan and immerse it in a bath of cold water. Occasionally swirl the wort in the pan and stir the cooling water around the pan. Depending on the volume and temperature of the water bath, change the water if necessary. Once the pan is comfortable to touch, give a final strong swirl to settle the hop debris and break material and let it rest for a further 10 minutes.

5. Pour the cooled wort off the hop debris and break material into a sanitized fermenter. Next add the can of malt extract and then 11 quarts (10 liters) of pre-boiled, cooled water. Check the temperature, gravity and volume, making any adjustments if necessary. Pitch the yeast when the temperature is around 64°F (18°C). Fit an airlock and keep the fermenter in a dark place at a constant 61° to 70°F (16° to 21°C). After primary fermentation, which should take 5 to 7 days, rack the beer of the sediment to a secondary fermenter (preferably a glass carboy). Keep the secondary fermenter in the same conditions as before until bubbles stop rising from the mixture (2 to 6 weeks). Bulk prime before bottling with 4.5 ounces (130 g) of sucrose for 24 quarts (23 liters).

OATMEAL STOUT

Oatmeal stout is a popular beer for many home brewers, especially for those that have tried a few kit bitters and now want to try something just a little more challenging. The stout body is hard to achieve with extract beers, but in this recipe you can appreciate how the oats provide a silky smoothness, the black patent malt enhances the color and gives a toasty character and the crystal malt adds body, sweetness and mouthfeel to the beer. The crystal malt also helps with head retention in the beer.

This is a malt extract with a steeped grains recipe rather than a partial mash. Ingredients for a 21-quart (20-liter) batch should come in at 7 percent ABV.

Ingredients

1 lb (0.5 kg) crystal malt, 120 L
1 lb (0.5 kg) black patent malt
2 lb (1 kg) flaked oats
3.5 lb (1.5 kg) amber dry malt extract
3.5 lb (1.5 kg) dark dry malt extract
2 oz (60 g) Northdown hops
0.5 oz (20 g) Fuggles hops
English ale yeast
2.5 oz (70 g) cane sugar, for bottle
    conditioning

Method

1. Steep all of the grains contained within a sparge bag in 5 quarts (5 liters) of cold water and bring to a boil. Simmer for 15 minutes and pour into the wort pot.

2. Wash grains through with cold water. Bring volume up to 8 quarts (8 liters) and add the malt extract and Northdown hops. Boil for 45 minutes and then add the Fuggles hops.

3. Boil for 15 minutes and allow to cool. Sparge with enough water to bring the volume to 21 quarts (20 liters). Ferment with English ale yeast in the usual manner.

4. When bottling, bulk prime with 2.5 ounces (70 grams) of cane sugar.

ESB—A PARTIAL MASH RECIPE

Extra Special Bitter has an ABV of 5.5 percent; the following recipe makes a 21-quart (20-liter) batch. This is a true partial mash, where surplus diastatic power of the malt extract is used to convert the malts that do not have enzymes. The Belgian biscuit malt will provide a warm bread or biscuit flavor and aroma.

Ingredients

4 lb (2 kg) British pale
14 oz (0.4 kg) crystal, 40 L
14 oz (0.4 kg) crystal, 60 L
10 oz (0.3 kg) Belgian biscuit malt
3.5 lb (1.5 kg) liquid light malt extract
1.25 oz (35 g) Challenger
0.75 oz (24 g) Kent Goldings
3.25 oz (85 g) cane sugar, for bottle
    conditioning

Method

1. Bring 11 quarts (10 liters) of strike water to 167°F (75°C). Add the grains and make sure mash stays at a constant 149°F (65°C) for 60 minutes. Halfway through the mash (30 minutes) begin heating 8 quarts (8 liters) sparge water to 167°F (75°C). Collect approx 8 quarts (8 liters) from the first runnings. Then sparge and collect second runnings. You should end up with about 16 quarts (15 liters) of pre-boil wort. This figure considers an evaporation loss.

2. Bring the wort to the boil. When boiling add the malt extract and 1 ounce (30 grams) of Challenger and 0.5 ounce (15 grams) of Kent Goldings hops. Boil for 60 minutes. Fifteen minutes before the end of the boil, add 0.2 ounce (5 grams) of Challenger and 0.3 ounce (9 grams) of Kent Goldings hops.After the boil cool as quickly as possible.

3. Ferment using an ale yeast in the usual manner. After the primary fermentation (about 5 to 7 days), it may be wise to transfer to a secondary fermenter for 2 weeks due to the amount of trub produced.

4. Bulk prime with 3.25 ounces (85 grams) of cane sugar.

THE VARIABLE BITTERNESS OF HOPS

You will find most packages of hops state the alpha acid percentage (AA%). This is because the AA% for any hop variety will vary due to growing conditions and other factors. Therefore if you brew two bitters to the same recipe with the same amount of Fuggles hops but the alpha acid content of one batch of hops was 4% and the other 6%, then there would be a noticable difference in the beers.

Some beer recipes not only specify the amount of hops used but also the alpha acid content. For the newcomer to brewing it is best not to worry about the alpha acid content, but just use the right amount of the correct hop. Your beer will be perfectly drinkable. The alpha acid content should only be of concern to the commercial brewer who needs consistant results with every batch of beer, or the advanced home brewer seeking to produce an award winner.

BEER RECIPES

BRITISH AND AMERICAN ALES

ORDINARY BITTER

This is a simple all-extract recipe. The recipe is easy and reliable, the ingredients cheap and easy to obtain. This is a good first step on from a kit and although ordinary by name, the resulting beer should still be superior to many mass-produced beers.

For 9.5 quarts (9 liters):

Ingredients
2 lb (900 g) liquid malt extract
13 oz (370 g) cane sugar
1.25 oz (35 g) Goldings hops
Ale yeast

Method
1. Boil 1 ounce (30 grams) of Goldings hops, contained in a sparge bag, then add 5 quarts (5 liters) of water for 45 minutes. Remove pan from the heat and leave for 5 minutes. Remove hops (squeeze as much water from them as possible).

2. Stir 2 pounds (900 grams) of malt extract and 12 ounces (340 grams) of cane sugar into this hopped water. Return pan to the heat and simmer for 5 minutes.

3. Put the hopped wort into a fermentation bucket and top up to 9.5 quarts (9 liters).

THE LOVIBOND SCALE

Crystal malts and various other speciality malts can vary widely in color. These are graded by the Lovibond scale, a system developed by British brewer Joseph Williams Lovibond. Each type of specialty grain is given a number followed by the letter "L." The higher the number translates into the depth of the color. For example, crystal malt 10 L adds minimal color and a slight caramel flavor. Crystal malt 60 L adds an amber color and increased caramel flavor. Crystal malt 120 L adds a deep reddish color and a rich, highly caramelized flavor. At the far end of the scale, black patent malt, 500 L, is the darkest colored malt and used in porters and stouts.

4. Check the temperature and when it is around 70°F (21°C) pitch in an ale yeast.

5. Three days in to the fermentation, stir in 0.2 ounces (5 grams) of Goldings hops. Dunk the hops well in to the brew so they are wet and do not float on top.

6. After fermentation has finished, move to a cold place for 2 days—this will help the

beer to clear. Rack the beer into a bottling bucket, then stir in and dissolve 1 ounce (30 grams) of cane sugar.

7. Bottle leaving a 2-in (5-cm) gap between cap and top of liquid.

───•••◦◦•••───

KENTISH PREMIUM BITTER

A grain with extract recipe. A Kentish-style bitter, with a good, pronounced hoppy flavor. This will produce 24 quarts (23 liters).

Ingredients
2 lb (1 kg) pale malt
4 oz (120 g) amber malt
10 oz (280 g) crystal malt 50–60 L
12 oz (340 g) torrefied wheat
1 oz (30 g) Challenger hops
1 oz (30 g) Goldings hops
1 tsp gelatin
Ale yeast
3 oz (80 g) cane sugar, for bottle
    conditioning

Method
1. Steep all of the grains in a large bag in 11 quarts (10 liters) of water. Bring the temperature up to 149°F (65°C) for 60 minutes. Remove the grains and top up to 19 quarts (18 liters).

2. Then add the following ingredients and boil this wort for 60 minutes:
    4 lb (2 kg) light dry malt extract

2 oz (60 g) glucose syrup
1 oz (30 g) Target hops

3. 15 minutes before the end of the boil add:
    0.5 oz (15 g) Challenger hops
    0.5 oz (15 g) Goldings hops

4. 5 minutes before the end of the boil add the remaining:
    0.5 oz (15 g) Challenger hops
    0.5 oz (15 g) Goldings hops

5. Chill the wort to around 68°F (20°C), transfer to primary fermenter and add ale yeast.

6. Add 1 tsp of gelatin when the brew has been transferred to a secondary fermenter.

7. Prime with 3 ounces (80 grams) of cane sugar that has been boiled in 8 fl oz (250 ml) of water.

───•••◦◦•••───

PREMIUM BITTER

An all-malt recipe for a premium bitter. For 11 quarts (10 liters):

Ingredients
3.5 lb (1.5 kg) liquid amber malt extract
0.5 lb (227 g) Amber dry malt extract
1.25 oz (35 g) Goldings hops
1 oz (30 g) Cascade hops
1 tsp gelatin
Ale yeast

1.5 oz (40 g) dried malt extract for bottle conditioning

Method

1. Boil the liquid amber malt extract, 0.5 lb (227g) amber dry malt extract and the Cascade hops in 3 quarts (3 liters) of water for 60 minutes (containing the hops in a sparge bag).

2. 10 minutes before the end of the boil add:
14 g Goldings hops

3. 5 minutes before the end of boil add another:
0.5 oz (14 g) Goldings hops

4. Strain off the hops, put the wort in the fermentation vessel and top up to 11 quarts (10 liters) with pre-boiled water at room temperature. Add ale yeast and 1 tsp of gelatin.

5. Fermentation should take about 5 to 7 days. After fermentation is complete, dry hops with 0.3 ounce (7 grams) of Goldings hops for 24 hours.

6. To carbonate, add 1.5 ounces (40 grams) of dried malt extract that has been boiled in 8 fl oz (250 ml) of water and allowed to cool, to the priming bucket.

LONDON-STYLE EXTRA SPECIAL BITTER

ESB is a favorite type of bitter among beer lovers. Here is an attempt to replicate a certain champion beer with a fuller taste.

Ingredients

In 24 quarts (23 liters) of water, steep:
21 oz (600 g) pale malt
6 oz (180 g) Carastan light malt 30 L
9.5 oz (270 g) crystal malt 70 to 80 L

for 45 minutes at 167°F (75°C)

Then add:
4 lb (2 kg) light liquid malt extract
3 lb (1.3 kg) liquid amber malt extract
1.5 oz (40 g) amber dry malt extract
1 oz (27 g) Fuggles hops
0.5 oz (22 g) Goldings hops

and boil for 60 minutes.

Method

1. Add 1 ounce (27 grams) of Fuggles 30 minutes before the end of boil and then 0.3 ounce (10 grams) of Goldings 5 minutes before the end of boil. Use an ESB yeast if you can get hold of one.

2. Dry hops with 0.4 ounce (12 grams) of Goldings in the secondary fermenter.

3. Carbonate with 1.5 ounces (40 grams) of dried malt extract that has been boiled in 8 fl oz (250 ml) of water and allowed to cool, to the priming bucket.

Note: Carastan is a British malt similar to American or Belgian crystal malts.

PALE ALES

Pale ales helped to change the face of brewing early in the 19th century. The new technologies of the Industrial Revolution enabled brewers to use pale malts to fashion beers that were genuinely golden or pale bronze in color. They were first brewed in London and Burton-on-Trent for the colonial markets. India Pale Ales (IPAs) were strong in alcohol and high in hops. The preservative character of the hops helped keep the beers in good condition during long sea journeys. Beers with less alcohol and hops were developed for the domestic market, and these were known simply as Pale Ales.

ORIGINAL PALE ALE

This is an extract recipe of the original type of Pale Ale.

Ingredients

    3.5 oz (100 g) flaked corn
    1 oz (30 g) Hallertau hops
    2 lb (900 g) light malt extract
    7 oz (200 g) glucose chips
    1 oz (30 g) cane sugar
    Ale yeast

Method

1. Boil the flaked corn in 5 quarts (5 liters) of water with the hops. Strain into a bucket, rinsing through the hops and corn with a little hot water.

2. Stir in the light malt extract and glucose chips. Top up with pre-boiled, cooled water to 9.5 quarts (9 liters). Add ale yeast when the temperature is around 70°F (21°C).

3. After fermentation has finished, move to a cold place for 2 days. Rack the beer into a bottling bucket, then stir in and dissolve 1 ounce (30 grams) of cane sugar.

INDIA PALE ALE

This is an extract recipe.

Ingredients

    6.5 lb (3 kg) light dry malt extract (1.5 ounces ,40 grams, to carbonate)
    2 oz (65 g) Fuggles
    2 oz (65 g) Willamette
    Ale yeast

Method

1. Boil 6.5 lb (3 kg) dry malt extract with 1.5 ounces (45 grams) of Fuggles in 13 quarts (12 liters) of water for 60 minutes.

2. 45 minutes before the end of boil, add the remaining 0.5 ounce (20 grams) of Fuggles.

3. 30 minutes before end of boil add 1 ounce (32 grams) of Willamette hops.

4. 5 minutes before end of boil add another ounce (32 grams) of Willamette.

5. Put hopped wort into fermenting bucket and top up to 21 quarts (20 liters).

6. Pitch in ale yeast when around 70°F (21°C).

7. Carbonate with 1.5 ounces (40 grams) of dried malt extract that has been boiled in 8 fl oz (250 ml) of water and allowed to cool, to the priming bucket. Bottle leaving a 2 in (5 cm) gap between cap and top of liquid.

SUMMERTIME IPA

This is an all grain recipe for IPA. It does take a while for the yeast to clear, but it seems to clear faster in the bottle than in the secondary, so use the secondary for a few days as a dry hop tun.

Ingredients

    9 lb (4 kg) pale malt
    10.5 oz (300 g) crystal malt
    7 oz (200 g) Carapils malt
    1.25 oz (35 g) Kent Goldings hops
    1 tsp Irish moss
    2 tsp gypsum
    2 oz (56 g) oak chips
    American ale yeast

Method

1. Mash pale malt at 153°F (67°C) for 30 to 60 minutes. Test after 30 minutes.

2. Add Crystal and Carapils and mash-out at 167°F (75°C) for 10 minutes. Sparge. Bring to boil.

3. In a saucepan, boil the oak chips for no more than 10 minutes, then strain the liquid into your boiling pot.

4. Add the gypsum and boil the wort. After 30 minutes of boiling add 0.5 ounce (14 grams) of hops.

5. After 45 minutes of boiling add another 0.5 ounce (14 grams) of hops and the Irish moss. Boil for a further 15 minutes.

6. Chill and pitch the yeast. Dry hop in the secondary fermenter with 0.3 ounce (7 grams) of hops. The beer will clear in the bottle.

ENGLISH MILD

This is an all-grain recipe for 24 quarts (23 liters) of traditional, dark mild ale with an ABV of 3.5 percent.

Ingredients

    6.5 lb (3 kg) pale malt
    0.5 lb (230 g) crystal malt 50–60 L
    6 oz (170 g) crystal malt 135–165 L
    2 oz (60 g) chocolate malt

0.5 oz (15 g) Willamette
0.5 oz (15 g) Fuggles
English ale yeast
1.75 oz (50 g) cane sugar, for bottle
  conditioning

Method

1. Mash all grains in 15 quarts (14 liters) of water at 153°F (67°C). Start starch tests after 50 minutes.

2. When ready, batch sparge with 13 quarts (12 liters) of water at 167°F (75°C).

3. Boil the wort with the Willamette hops for 60 minutes. 30 minutes into the boil, add the Fuggles.

4. Chill the wort, transfer to the fermenter and pitch the yeast when the correct temperature.

5. The primary fermetation should take 5 to 7 days. Leave in the same vessel for a further 7 days.
6. Bulk prime with 1.75 ounces (50 grams) of cane sugar—this style of beer should have a low carbonation.

———

NUT BROWN ALE

This is a partial mash recipe for 24 quarts (23 liters) of nut brown ale. It uses honey malt, which looks a lot like caramel malt but is processed in a different way, meaning there

isn't the sharpness associated with caramel. The process develops sugars and rich malt qualities that give it honey-like flavor.

Ingredients

3 lb (1.3 kg) American 2-row malt
1 lb (450 g) Munich
1 lb (450 g) honey malt
1 lb (450 g) crystal malt 50–60 L
6 oz (170 g) chocolate malt
6 lb (2.75 kg) light dry malt extract
3.25 oz (85 g) Fuggles
English ale yeast
2.5 oz (70 g) cane sugar, for bottle
  conditioning

Method

1. Mash all grains in 15 quarts (14 liters) of water at 153°F (67°C), start starch tests after 50 minutes.

2. When ready, batch sparge with 13 quarts (12 liters) of water at 167°F (75°C).

3. Add the wort to the boiler, add the malt extracta and 1.5 ounce (45 grams) of Fuggles and top up to 27 quarts (26 liters). Boil the wort for 60 minutes, 40 minutes into the boil add a further 1.5 ounce (40 grams) of Fuggles.

4. The primary fermentation should take 5 to 7 days. Leave in the same vessel for a further 7 days.

5. When bottling, bulk prime with 2.5 ounces (70 grams) of cane sugar.

ENGLISH OLD ALE

For 20 quarts (19 liters) of dark, old ale.

Ingredients

    6.5 lb (3 kg) dark liquid malt extract
    9 oz (250 g) corn sugar
    10 fl oz (300 ml) molasses
    1.5 oz (45 g) Czech Saaz hop pellets
    ¼ tsp Irish moss
    English ale yeast
    2 oz (60 g) cane sugar, for bottle
conditioning

Method

1. Boil 6 quarts (6 liters) of water, then add the malt extract, corn sugar, molasses and 1 ounce (30 grams) of hops. Return to a boil, and let it continue to boil for 15 minutes then add the Irish moss and boil for a further 10 minutes.

2. Remove from heat and add remaining 0.5 ounce (15 grams) of hops and let them steep for 2 minutes.

3. Add 8 quarts (8 liters) of pre-boiled cold water to the fermenting vessel and then strain the wort into the vessel.

4. Top up to 20 quarts (19 liters) and check and adjust temperature before pitching yeast.

5. Fit airlock and keep in a warm, dark place. Primary fermentation should take 5 to 7 days. Allow another 7 days for secondary fermentation.

6. When bottling, bulk prime with2 ounces (60 grams) of cane sugar.

—————

BARLEY WINE

This recipe using champagne wine yeast should produce 5 quarts (5 liters) of beer with an ABV of around 10 to 11 percent.

Ingredients

    2 lb (900 g) diastatic malt extract
    9 oz (250 g) pale malt
    9 oz (250 g) crystal malt
    3.5 oz (100 g) brown sugar
    Juice of a lemon
    0.75 oz (25 g) Goldings hops
    Champagne wine yeast
    0.5 oz (15 g) cane sugar, for bottle
      conditioning

Method

1. Heat 2 quarts (2 liters) of water to 167°F (75°C) and stir in the extract, pale and crystal malts.

2. Transfer to an insulated mash tun for 60 minutes.

3. Strain out the wort in a large pot and sparge the grains with another 2 quarts (2 liters) of water at 167°F (75°C).

4. Stir in the sugar, lemon juice and hops and boil for 60 minutes.

5. Remove from heat and leave for 15 minutes to allow the solids to settle.

6. Add the wort to the fermenter, straining through a sparge bag, add all the solids to the bag and rinse through with half a quart (half a liter) of water at 167°F (75°C). Press the solids to extract the diluted sugars.

7. Top the fermenter up to 5 quarts (5 liters).

8. Make up a yeast starter by removing 3 fl oz (100 ml) of the wort and diluting with 3 fl oz (100 ml) of pre-boiled cold water, add the yeast after checking the temperature is 97 to 104°F (36 to 40°C). Leave for 20 minutes.

9. Check the wort is around 68°F (20°C) and pitch the yeast. Transfer the bucket to a warm dark position.

10. The primary fermenation will probably be vigorous and take 1 to 2 days. When activity subsides rack off the brew to a demijohn.

11. Keep the demijohn in the same warm place for a further 12 days and check the gravity to ensure it is suitable for bottling.

12. Bulk prime with 0.5 ounce (15 grams) of cane sugar. Store bottles for 2 weeks at 68 to 77°F (20 to 25°C) and then, for 1 year, in a cool store.

SCOTTISH EXPORT ALE

True to its style, this beer has no finishing hops. Makes a 24-quart (23-liter) batch.

Ingredients

   6 lb (2.75 kg) amber dry malt extract

   1 lb (450 g) crystal malt 60 L

   0.5 lb (225 g) chocolate malt 340 L

   1 lb (450 g) dark brown sugar

   2 oz (60 g) Fuggles pelletized hops

   1 tsp Irish moss

   Ale yeast (Scottish ale yeast if available)

   3.5 oz (100 g) cane sugar, for bottle conditioning

Method

1. Pre-boil and cool 8 quarts (8 liters) of water and store in covered bucket.

2. Add 17 quarts (16 liters) of water to boiler and heat to 149°F (65°C). Remove from heat and steep crystal and chocolate malts for 15 minutes.

3. Return to heat and at around 167°F (75°C), remove malts. Add malt extract, brown sugar and Fuggles. Boil for 1 hour. For the last 15 minutes of boil, add Irish moss.

4. Cool wort and add to fermenter. Pitch yeast at 68°F (20°C). Keep in dark area at 68°F (20°C).

5. Primary should take 4 to 5 days. Keep in the fermenter for a further 5 to 7 days.

6. Bulk prime for bottling with 3.5 ounces (100 grams) of cane sugar.

IRISH STOUT

This is an all-grain full mash that will produce 24 quarts (23 liters) of fine stout at 4.3 percent ABV.

Ingredients

6.5 lb (3 kg) pilsner malt
2 lb (1 kg) flaked barley
18 oz (500 g) roasted barley
9 oz (250 g) wheat malt
6 oz (170 g) black patent malt
6 oz (170 g) chocolate malt
1.5 oz (43 g) Northern Brewer hops
Ale yeast
2.5 oz (72 g) cane sugar, for bottle
conditioning

Method

1. Two days before starting the mash, do a sour mash with 0.5 pound (225 grams) of the pilsner malt. Add the grains to 1 quart (1 liter) of water at 131°F (55°C) and allow to sour for 2 days.

2. On brew day, mash in with 12 quarts (11 liters) of water at 149°F (65°C) for 90 minutes. Add contents of the sour mash to this mash.

3. Increase the mash temperature to 167°F (75°C) for 10 minutes.

4. Sparge with 19 quarts (18 liters) of water at 167°F (75°C) collecting about 21 to 24 quarts (20-23 liters) of wort.

5. Add 1 ounce (28 grams) of hops to the wort and boil for 60 minutes. Add the remainder of the hops 30 minutes in to the boil.

6. Cool wort and pitch yeast when 68°F (20°C).

7. After a week in primary, rack off to a secondary fermenter. Bulk prime with 2.5 ounces (72 grams) of cane sugar, the aim being to keep the texture creamy, rather than fizzy.

PUMPKIN ALE

Thomas Jefferson brewed beer and this is based on one of his recipes. Yields 20 quarts (19 liters) of spicy, tasty beer that is best matured in the bottle for at least 3 months.

Ingredients

6.5 lb (3 kg) liquid amber malt extract
5 lb (2.25 kg) pumpkin
25 oz (700 g) pale malt
18 oz (500 g) crystal malt
1.75 oz (50 g) Willamette hops
1 oz (30 g) chopped root ginger
2 tsp ground cinnamon
1 tsp nutmeg
1 tsp gypsum
1 tsp Irish moss
Ale yeast
3.25 oz (90 g) cane sugar, for bottle
conditioning

Method

1. Rinse pumpkin, leave skin on and cut into large sections. Bake in 356°F (180°C) oven for 1 hour and 15 minutess, or until caramelized on the outside. Remove skin and crush meat.

2. Place pumpkin, gypsum and grains into a pot. Add 6 quarts (6 liters) of water and mash at 149°F (65°C) for 1 hour.

3. Strain into a bucket and sparge with 4 quarts (4 liters) of water at 167°F (75°C). Return the wort to the pot and boil. Add malt extract and 1 ounce (30 grams) of hops. Boil for 1 hour. Thirty minutes in to the boil add the Irish moss. At 50-minute mark, add remaining hops. At 55-minute mark, add the spices. Remove from heat and let it stand for 5 minutes.

4. Pour wort through a strainer into fermenting bucket with enough cold water to make 20 quarts (19 liters).

5. Pitch yeast when temperature is 77 to 8°F (25 to 27°C).

6. After rapid fermentation is complete, rack to a secondary containter and allow to finish. This beer must be racked once due to excessive trub.

7. Bottle when fermentation is complete. Bulk priming with 3.25 ouncces (90 grams) of cane sugar.

MAPLE PORTER

Ingredients

    5.5 lb (2.5 kg) light dry malt extract
    25 oz (700 g) crystal malt 60 L
    0.5 lb (225 g) black patent malt
    1 lb (450 g) maple syrup
    2.5 oz (70 g) Goldings hop pellets
    Ale yeast
    3.5 oz (100 g) cane sugar, for bottle
      conditioning

Method

1. Crush the malts and grains and put them into a sparge bag in a large pot. Steep in 11 quarts (10 liters) of cold water. Heat the water to 167°F (75°C), remove the bag and hold it over the pot untilthe liquid flows out of it.
2. Turn up the heat to bring the liquid to a boil. Add the dry malt extract and 1 ounce (30 grams) of hops.

3. Return to the boil, keep on a rolling boil for 60 minutes. Halfway through the boil add another ounce (30 grams) of hops. Forty-five minutes in to the boil, add the maple syrup and the remainder of the hops.

4. At the end of the boil, cool the wort down to fermentation temperature, transfer to the bucket, top up to 24 quarts (23 liters) and add the yeast.

5. After 5 to 7 days the primary fermentation should be over. Rack off the brew to a secondary fermenter for another 7 days.

6. Bottle when fermentation is complete. Bulk prime with 3.5 ounces (100 grams) of cane sugar.

BELGIAN BEERS

DUBBEL

A Trappist-style beer with a gentle flavor, creamy head and pronounced bouquet. Produces 20 quarts (19 liters) at 6.4 percent ABV.

Ingredients

6.5 lb (3 kg) light liquid malt extract

2 lb (1 kg) light dry malt extract

1 lb (450 g) Belgian candy sugar

4 oz (115 g) crystal malt 10 L

4 oz (115 g) brown malt

1 oz (28 g) Golding hops

0.5 oz (14 g) Hallertauer hops

½ tsp Irish moss

Trappist ale yeast

2.5 oz (74 g) cane sugar, for bottle conditioning

Method

1. Steep the crushed malted grains in 8 quarts (8 liters) of water at 149°F (65°C) for 30 minutes.

2. Remove the grain from the hot water with a strainer, then bring water to a boil. When boiling starts, remove pot from heat and add 1 pound (450 grams) liquid malt extract.

3. Return to a boil, then add Goldings hops and boil for 60 minutes.

4. Add Irish moss for last 45 minutes of boil.

5. Add Hallertauer hops for last 3 minutes of the boil.

6. At end of boil, add remainder of liquid malt extract syrup, the dry malt extract and candy sugar and stir to mix. Wait 10 minutes to sanitize.

7. Fill fermenter with 8 quarts (8 liters) of cold water. Strain the hot wort into the fermenter and top up to the 8-quart (8-liter) mark.

8. Add yeast when beer is less than 77°F (25°C).

9. Ferment at 70°F (21°C) for 5 to 7 days and then transfer to a secondary fermenter for 2 weeks.

10. Bulk prime with 2.5 ounces (74 grams) of cane sugar before bottling.

SPICED HONEY BEER

This beer, although based on malt extract, has hints of wheat beer about it. It is cloudy, spicy and refreshingly different. The recipe uses the malt extract technique for brewing and will produce 24 quarts (23 liters).

Ingredients

5.5 lb (2.5 kg) liquid light malt extract

0.5 oz (14 g) dried orange peel

1.25 oz (35 g) crushed whole coriander seed
2 lb (900 g) honey
3.25 oz (90 g) Hallertauer hops
Wheat beer yeast
4 oz (120 g) cane sugar, for bottle
   conditioning

Method

1. Bring 8 quarts (8 liters) of water to the boil and dissolve the malt extract, honey and 2 oz (60 g) of the hops. Boil for 45 minutes and then add further 0.5 oz (15 g) of hops and 0.5 oz (15 g) of the crushed coriander and boil for a further 10 minutes. Add the rest of the coriander and the orange peel and boil for a further 5 minutes. Add a further 0.5 oz (15 g) of the hops for another 2 mins.

2. Add 8 quarts (8 litets) of water to the fermenting bucket then strain the boiled liquid into the water. Top up the fermenting bucket to 24 quart (23-liter) mark. Add the yeast when the liquid is the correct temperature.

3. Place a clean tea towel over the top of the fermenting bucket then place the lid loosely on top. Move to a warm, dark area and leave until fermentation is complete.

4. Bottle and wait for around 2 weeks before drinking. This beer will have a cloudy appearance but this is normal.

5. Bottle when fermentation is complete. Bulk prime with 4 ounces (120 grams) of cane sugar.

BELGIAN LEFTY BLONDE

This recipe aims to replicate one of the world's finest beers.

Ingredients

   European lager kit for 22 quarts (21 liters)
   3.5 lb (1.5 kg) pale malt extract
   18 oz (500 g) liquid glucose
   0.75 oz (25 g) Saaz hop pellets
   Ale yeast

Method

1. Boil 2 quarts (2 liters) of water and add the malt and glucose. Turn down the heat to a simmering temperature while stirring the mixture until everything is disolved.

2. Add the hops to the mix and simmer for a further minute.

3. Pour the lager kit into the fermenter followed by the boiled mix.

4. Top up with 22 quarts (21 liters) and when cool enough add the yeast.

5. Brew out as per the instructions on the kit, typically 7 to 14 days.

BELGIAN TRAPPIST WHITE BEER

This beer is strong yet light, very carbonated, and just slightly bitter.

Ingredients

    10 lb (4.5 kg) Pilsner malt
    1 lb (450 g) wheat malt
    4 oz (115 g) rice hulls
    24 oz (680 g) cane sugar
    1 tsp lemon juice
    2 oz (55 g) Goldings hops
    1 oz (27 g) Hallertrau Hersbrucker hops
    Belgian ale yeast
    4.75 oz (135 g) cane sugar, for bottle
      conditioning

Method

1. Heat the sugar with a small amount of water (enough to make a syrup) and a teaspoon of lemon juice. The lemon juice will help invert the sugar into simpler sugars. After about 15 minutes the sugar will turn a very light yellow color.

2. Mash the grains for 90 minutes in an insulated mash tun in 8 quarts (8 liters) of water at 149°F (65°C).

3. Batch sparge with a further 8 quarts (8 liters) of water at 167°F (75°C).

4. Add the sugar syrup created earlier and 1.5 ounces (42 grams) of the Goldings and 0.5 ounce (14 grams) of the Hallertrau at the start of boil. Boil the wort for 90 minutes. Five minutes before the end of the boil, add the remaining hops.

5. Chill and strain into a fermenter and top up to 24 quarts (23 liters). Ferment at 70°F (21°C) for 5 to 7 days and then transfer to a secondary fermenter for 2 weeks.

6. Bulk prime with 4.57 ounces (135 grams) of cane sugar before bottling. This beer benefits from being left to mature for at least 3 months.

A BELGIAN WIT BIER

A wheat beer, perfect for slaking a thirst after a bit of work in the garden on a summer's day. Makes 24 quarts (23 liters) of beer with an ABV of 5.5 percent.

Ingredients

    3.5 lb (1.5 kg) light liquid malt extract
    2 lb (1 kg) dry wheat malt extract
    0.5 lb (225 g) cracked unmalted wheat
    0.5 lb (225 g) flaked oats
    1 oz (28 g) Saaz hops
    0.5 oz (20 g) Goldings hops
    1 tsp crushed coriander seeds
    Zest of 2 oranges, excluding pith
    Belgian wit yeast
    6.5 oz (190 g) cane sugar, for bottle
      conditioning

Method

1. Steep whole grains inside a sparge bag in 2 quarts (2 liters) of water at 149°F (65°C) for 30 minutes.

2. Rinse through with 1 quart (1 liter) of water at 167°F (75°C).

3. Remove grains and add 8 quarts (8 liters) of water, the extracts, 0.5 ounce (15 grams) of Saaz and 0.5 ounce (15 grams) of Goldings and boil for 60 minutes.

4. 45 minutes after start of boil, add another 0.5 ounce (15 grams) of Saaz, the coriander seeds and orange zest.

5. Chill and strain into a fermenter, top up to 24 quarts (23 liters). Add yeast and ferment at 70°F (21°C) for 14 days.

6. Bulk prime with 6.5 ounces (190 grams) of cane sugar before bottling.

WIT BIER WITH ZING

A simple, extract with grain recipe for 20 quarts (19 liters) of a wit bier with zing. ABV of 5.5 percent.

Ingredients

    4 oz (120 g) wheat malt
    1 lb (450 g) crystal malt 10 L
    3.5 lb (1.5 kg) light liquid malt extract
    3.5 lb (1.5 kg) wheat extract
    1 oz (28 g) Northern brewer
    1 oz (28 g) Cascade hops
    Juice and zest of 2 whole lemons
    1 tsp ground ginger
    Belgian wit yeast

6 oz (175 g) cane sugar, for bottle
    conditioning

Method

1. Steep whole grains inside a sparge bag in 4 quarts (4 liters) of water at 149°F (65°C) for 30 minutes.

2. Rinse through with 2 quarts (2 liters) of water at 167°F (75°C).

3. Remove grains and add the extracts, the Northern brewer hops and top up the water to 12 quarts (11 liters), and boil for 60 minutes.

4. Add the Cascade hops and the ginger to the hop bag 5 minutes before the end of boil.

5. Add the juice of 2 lemons, 2 minutes before end of boil.

6. Chill wort and strain into a fermenter, top up to 20 quarts (19 liters). Add yeast and the zest (no pith) of 2 lemons in a hop bag and ferment at 70°F (21°C) for 14 days.

7. Carbonate by bulk priming with 6 ounces (175 grams) of cane sugar before bottling.

RASPBERRY BEER

Framboise has become popular outside of Belgium, and can now be found in pubs and supermarkets all over the world. This is an attempt at giving something of the taste of a Framboise beer. An extract with grain recipe, it will yield 16 quarts (15 liters) with an of ABV 5.5 percent.

Ingredients
3.5 lb (1.5 kg) crystal malt 40 L
0.5 lb (225 g) dextrine malt (Cara-Pils)
3 lb (1.3 kg) light dry malt extract
12 oz (340 g) cane sugar
2 lb (1 kg) raspberries, washed
1 oz (28 g) Goldings
Belgian ale yeast
6 oz (170 g) cane sugar, for bottle conditioning

Method
1. Steep crystal malt in 8 quarts (8 liters) of water at 149°F (65°C) water for 45 minutes.

2. Add dry malt extract, dextrine and 0.5 ounce (14 grams) of hops and boil for 40 minutes.

3. After the 40 minute boil, add sugar, raspberries, and remainder of hops and boil for another 10 minutes.

4. Chill and strain into a fermenter, top off at 16 quarts (15 liters). Add yeast, ferment at 70°F (21°C) for 5 to 7 days, rack into secondary fermenter when activity slows.

5. After 5 to 7 days in secondary, bulk prime with 6 ounces (170 grams) of cane sugar and bottle.

BREWING LAGER

Lagers can take months to craft and may require some sort of refrigeration to produce a good quality beer. The novice home brewer would be best advised to start out with a beer, such as a pale ale, porter, or stout, which uses ale yeast for fermentation.

Lager yeasts are more successful at lower temperatures than those used for brewing ales, typically 46 to 57°F (8 to 14°C), and flocculate closer to the bottom of the fermentation tank. Because of the lower temperatures, lager yeasts also tend to take longer to ferment fully. When the lager yeasts have finished fermenting they leave behind less residual sweetness and flavor than ales. Lagers are also aged at much lower temperatures than ales, around 37 to 46°F (3 to 8°C), and for a much longer time, typically months. This is called lagering and creates a cleaner, clearer beer.

GRAND CRU

A recipe for a rich, dark, wine-like beer with an ABV of 8 percent. Produces 20 quarts (19 liters).

Ingredients

  6.5 lb (3 kg) light liquid malt extract
  0.5 lb (225 g) pale malt
  2 lb (1 kg) crystal malt 10 L
  1 lb (450 g) Belgian candy sugar
  1 lb (450 g) corn sugar
  Peel of 1 orange (no pith)
  0.5 oz (20 g) crushed coriander seeds
  3 oz (77 g) Sterling hops
  Belgian abbey ale yeast
  0.3 oz (8 g) cane sugar, for bottle
    conditioning

Method

1. Steep the crushed malts in 13 quarts (12 liters) of water at 149°F (65°C) for 30 minutes. Remove grains from wort, add 18 ounces (500 grams) of the malt extract, and bring to a boil.

2. Add 1.5 ounces (42 grams) of hops and the orange peel and boil for 60 minutes. Add the candy sugar, corn sugar and coriander with the remainder of the hops for the last 5 minutes of the boil. Add the remainder of the malt extract at the end of the boil and let steep for 5 minutes to sanitize.

3. Now add the wort to 8 quarts (8 liters) of cool water in a sanitary fermenter, and top up with cool water to 21 quarts (20 liters). Cool the wort to 73°F (23°C) and pitch the yeast. Allow the beer to cool over the next few hours to 70°F (21°C), and hold at this temperature until the beer has finished fermenting. Hold the beer at 66°F (19°C) for 3 days. Then cool the beer to 36 to 43°F (2 to 6°C) for a further 3 days to drop the yeast out of suspension and clear the beer.

4. Bulk prime with 0.3 ounce (8 grams) of cane sugar and bottle.

GERMAN AND CZECH BEERS

BOHEMIAN PILSNER

A tasty and easy-to-drink beer. This recipe produces 20 quarts (19 liters) at 4.3 percent ABV.

Ingredients

  6.5 lb (3 kg) light liquid malt extract
  0.5 lb (225 g) crystal malt 20 L
  1 lb (450 g) pilsner malt
  0.5 lb (225 g) Dextrin malt
  4 oz (112 g) Sterling hops
  1 tsp Irish moss
  Pilsner yeast
  3.75 oz (110 g) cane sugar, for bottle
    conditioning

Method

1. Steep crushed malted grain in 8 quarts (8 liters) of water at 149°F (65°C) for 30 minutes.

2. Remove the grain from the hot water with a strainer, then bring water to a boil.

3. Remove pot from burner and add 1.75 ounces (50 grams) of liquid malt extract. Return to a boil, then add 2 ounces (56 grams) of hops and Irish moss and boil for 45 minutes.

4. Add 1 ounce (28 grams) of hops for the last 30 minutes of the boil. Add remainder of hops for the last 15 minutes of the boil.

5. At the end of boil add remainder of malt extract and stir gently. Wait 10 minutes to sanitize.

6. Fill your fermenter with 8 quarts (8 liters) of cold water. Strain the hot wort into the bucket and top up to 20 quarts (19 liters).

7. Add yeast when beer is less than 75°F (24°C), and ferment at 50 to 60°F (10 to 15°C). Because of the cooler temperatures, expect fermentation to take longer—it could be about 3 to 4 weeks.

8. Bulk prime with 3.75 ounces (110 grams) of cane sugar before bottling.

WEIZEN

This beer is typical of Berlin-style wheat beers. The recipe yields 24 quarts (23 liters).

Ingredients

3.5 lb (1.5 kg) liquid amber malt extract
3 lb (1.3 kg) light dry malt extract
3 lb (1.3 kg) wheat malt
1.5 oz (42 g) Hallertau hops
0.3 oz (9 g) Willamette hops
1 Tbsp gypsum
Ale yeast
5 oz (140 g) cane sugar, for bottle conditioning

Method

1. Heat 3 quarts (3 liters) of water to 167°F (75°C) and add grains and gypsum. Mash for 1 hour, maintaining a temperature of 149°F (65°C).

2. Strain out grains, pouring water into second pot.

3. Heat 2 quarts (2 liters) of water to 167°F (75°C) and use it to rinse the grains.

4. Add all the extract (liquid and dry) and the Hallertau hops. Boil for 30 minutes.

5. Add Willamette hops during last 2 minutes of the boil.

6. Put 8 quarts (8 liters) of water into fermenter and add hot wort. Top up so that the total volume is 24 quarts (23 liters). Pitch the yeast when wort temperature is 77 to 81°F (25 to 27°C), cover, and attach airlock.

7. Ferment for 10 days, rack and ferment for a further 4 days.

8. Bulk prime with 5 ounces (140 grams) of cane sugar before bottling.

MÄRZENBIER

In 16th-century Bavaria, due to the hot weather, brewing ended with the coming of spring, and began again in the fall. Most beers were brewed in March (*Märzen*). These brews were kept in cold storage over the spring and summer months, or brewed at a higher gravity, so they'd keep. Märzenbier is full-bodied, rich, toasty, typically dark copper in color with a medium to high alcohol content. The following extract with grains recipe produces 20 quarts (19 liters).

Ingredients

- 0.5 lb (225 g) Munich malt
- 0.5 lb (225 g) carapils malt
- 3.5 lb (1.5 kg) pale dry malt extract
- 3.5 lb (1.5 kg) amber dry malt extract
- 1.5 oz (42 g) Tettnang hops
- 0.5 oz (20 g) Saaz hops
- Lager yeast
- 3.25 oz (90 g) cane sugar, for bottle conditioning

Method

1. Steep the Munich and carapils malts in a sparge bag, in 11 quarts (10 liters) of water at 149°F (65°C) for 45 minutes.

2. Remove grains and add the dry malt extract to the water, bring to a boil and add the Tettnang hops in a hop bag.

3. Boil for 60 minutes. After the boil, remove from the heat and add the Saaz hops. After 30 minutes remove the hops from the wort.

4. Top up to 20 quarts (19 liters) with chilled, pre-boiled water and cool the wort.

5. When around 61°F (16°C), pitch the yeast.

6. Ferment at 50°F (10°C) for 1 week, move to a cooler location (41°F, 5°C, if possible) for 2 weeks, then transfer to secondary and condition cold (27° to 41°F, 3° to 5°C) for 6 to 8 weeks.

7. Bulk prime with 3.25 ounces (90 grams) of cane sugar before bottling. Let it mature for at least 2 months.

PALE BOCK

Bocks were dark lagers, traditionally brewed for special occasions, often religious festivals such as Christmas, Easter or Lent. Modern Bocks can be dark, amber or pale in color. This is a recipe for 20 quarts (19 liters) of pale bock at around 6.2 percent ABV.

Ingredients

- 7 lb (3.25 kg) pale liquid malt extract
- 0.5 lb (225 g) aromatic malt
- 0.5 lb (225 g) carapils malt
- 0.5 lb (225 g) caramel malt 10 L
- 2 oz (56 g) Cascade hops
- 1.5 oz (44 g) Chinook hops
- 1 tsp Irish moss
- Bock lager yeast
- 3.25 oz (90 g) cane sugar, for bottle conditioning

Method

1. Add grains to 8 quarts (8 liters) of water. Bring slowly to 167°F (75°C)

.

2. Remove grains and bring liquid to a boil. When boiling, add liquid malt extract and Cascade hops. Boil for 60 minutes.

3. 30 minutes into the boil, add Irish moss and 1 ounce (30 grams) of Chinook hops.

4. At end of boil, turn off heat, remove hops and transfer to fermenting container. Top up to 20 quarts (19 liters). Pitch yeast at 70°F (21°C).

5. Ferment for 3 days and rack to secondary. Add 0.5 ounce (14 grams) of Chinook hops to secondary fermenter.

6. Ferment for 3 weeks at 61°F (16°C).

7. Bulk prime with 3.25 ounces (90 grams) of cane sugar before bottling.

EISBOCK

Eisbocks gain their strength from being frozen at the end of their maturation period. Ice is then taken away from the brew and as a result, the alcohol concentration in the beer increases. You will, of course, need a large freezer to perform this process. The result will be a beer of around 10 percent ABV.

Ingredients

25 oz (700 g) CaraMunich malt
8 lb (3.5 kg) liquid amber malt extract
3.5 lb (1.5 kg) liquid dark malt extract
2 oz (56 g) Hallertauer hops
1 tsp Irish moss
Bock lager yeast
2 oz (60 g) cane sugar, for bottle conditioning

Method

1. Steep the grains, in a sparge bag, in 8 quarts (8 liters) of water at 149°F (65°C) for 45 minutes.

2. Remove grains and bring liquid to a boil. When boiling, add malt extract syrups and 1 ounce (28 grams) of hops. Boil 60 minutes.

3. After 45 minutes of boiling, add the remainder of hops and the Irish moss.
4. At end of boil, turn off heat, remove hops and transfer to fermenting container. Top up to 20 quarts (19 liters). Pitch yeast at 70°F (21°C).

5. Ferment for 3 days and rack to secondary. Ferment in secondary for 3 weeks at 61°F (16°C).

6. Freeze to remove 5 quarts (5 liters) of water as ice. This process of removing ice should leave around 13 quarts (12 liters) of Eisbock.

7. Bulk prime with 2 ounces (60 grams) of cane sugar before bottling.

SCHWARZBIER

Schwarzbier (black beer) is often referred to as a Schwarzpils, a "black Pils," but, unlike a blond Pils, which can be quite bitter, the hop bitterness in Schwarzbier is gentle and subdued. This is an extract with grain recipe that produces 20 quarts (19 liters) of beer at around 5 percent ABV.

Ingredients

4 oz (120 g) Carapils malt
0.5 lb (230 g) CaraMunich malt
4 oz (120 g) chocolate malt
2 oz (60 g) black patent
3.5 lb (1.5 kg) liquid light malt extract
3 lb (1.3 kg) light dry malt extract
1 oz (28 g) Northern Brewer
1 oz (28 g) Hallertauer Hersbrucker
1 tsp Irish moss
Lager yeast
3.75 oz (110 g) cane sugar, for bottle
   conditioning

Method

1. Steep grains in 8 quarts (8 liters) of water for 60 minutes at 167°F (75°C).

2. Rinse through grains with 4 quarts (4 liters) of water at 167°F (75°C).

3. Bring liquid to a boil. When boiling, add malt extracts and the Northern Brewer hops and boil for 60 minutes.

4. 15 minutes before end of boil, add the Hallertauer hops.

OBTAINING YEAST FROM BOTTLE CONDITIONED BEER

You may find it hard to find a suitable yeast for beers like Weizenbier or Trappist ales. If you cannot get the right yeast from your homebrew supplier, the yeast layer from bottle conditioned beers can be harvested and grown just like the yeast from a liquid yeast packet.

Find bottle conditioned beer of the same style that you wish to brew.

Sanitize equipment. Make a starter solution by stirring 1.75 ounces (50 grams) of light dry malt extract (DME) into 13.5 fl oz (400 ml) of water and boiling for 20 minutes. Allow to cool to pitching temperature.

Open the bottle of beer and thoroughly clean the bottle neck and opening with sanitizer to prevent contamination.

Pour the beer into a glass, leaving a small amount of beer and the yeast in the bottle. Swirl up the sediment with the beer remaining in the bottle and pour the yeast sediment into the starter solution.

You may need the yeast from 2 to 3 bottles for the starter.

Keep the starter for 2 days at a suitable fermenting temperature before pitching into wort.

5. 5 minutes before end of boil, add the Irish moss.

6. At end of boil, turn off heat, remove hops and transfer to fermenting vessel. Top up to 20 quarts (19 liters). Pitch yeast at 70°F (21°C).

7. Ferment for 1 week at 61°F (16°C). Transfer to secondary for 3 weeks at 50°F (10°C).

8. Bulk prime with 3.75 ounces (110 grams) of cane sugar before botttling.

9. Condition bottles for 1 week at room temperature and then 5 days at 41°F (5°C).

—————

DUNKELWEIZEN

Dunkelweizens are dark wheat beers that usually include either Vienna or Munich malts in the ingredients. These malts contribute a chestnut brown color and are the primary malts used the Oktoberfest style.

Ingredients
- 6 lb (2.75 kg) wheat malt
- 4 lb (1.8 kg) Munich malt
- 1 lb (450 g) CaraMunich 60 L
- 0.5 oz (14 g) Hallertauer Herbrucker hops
- 0.5 oz (14 g) Tettnang hops
- Weizen yeast
- 6 oz (180 g) cane sugar, for bottle conditioning

Method

1. Mix the crushed grains in the tun and slowly pour on 8 quarts (8 liters) of water at 167°F (75°C). Let the temperature stabilize at 149°F (65°C) and mash for 90 minutes, stirring every 15 minutes.

2. Sparge through with 11 quarts (10 liters) of water at 167°F (75°C).

3. Sparge through a second time with enough water at 167°F (75°C) to bring the amount in the boiler to 24 quarts (23 liters).

4. Boil the wort for 30 minutes.

5. Add the Hallertauer hops and boil for 30 minutes more.

6. Add the Tettnang hops and boil for another 30 minutes.

7. Cool the wort to room temperature and rack off, into a fermenter.

8. When wort is 70°F (21°C), pitch the yeast.

9. Let ferment at 66°F (19°C) for 10 days. Rack and let ferment at 66°F (19°C) for another week.

10. Bulk prime with 6 ounces (180 grams) of cane sugar before botttling.

11. Condition bottles for 1 week at room temperature and then 5 days at 41°F (5°C).

FRENCH BEER

BIÈRE DE GARDE

A style from the Pas-de-Calais region of France, Bière de Garde, or "keeping beer," is traditionally a strong, top fermenting, bottle conditioned brew. Today it is often bottom fermented and filtered.

Ingredients
12 lb (5.5 kg) Vienna malt
12 oz (350 g) Belgian aromatic malt
9 oz (250 g) white wheat malt
7 oz (200 g) brown sugar
6 oz (170 g) Belgian Special B malt
1 oz (28 g) Mount Hood hops
1 oz (28 g) Spalter hops
1 oz (28 g) Sterling hops
Bière de Garde yeast
3.5 oz (100 g) brown sugar, for bottle
conditioning

Method
1. Mash grains in 8 quarts (8 liters) of water at 145°F (63°C) for 30 minutes. Heat to 151°F (66°C) and stand for 40 minutes.

2. Rinse through grains with 13 quarts (12 liters) of water at 167°F (75°C).

3. Bring liquid to a boil. When boiling, add 1 ounce (28 grams) of Mount Hood hops and boil for 60 minutes.

4. Fifteen minutes before the end of the boil, add 1 oz (28 g) of Spalter hops and 0.5 oz (14 g) of Sterling hops.

5. Five minutes before end of boil, add the remainder of hops and the brown sugar.

6. At end of boil, turn off heat, remove hops and transfer to fermenting vessel. Top up to 20 quarts (19 liters). Pitch yeast at 70°F (21°C).

7. Ferment for 2 weeks at 70°F (21°C). Transfer to secondary for 3 weeks at 70°F (21°C).

8. Bulk prime with 3.5 ounces (100 grams) of brown sugar before bottling. Store in a cool, dark place for at least 2 months.

BALTIC PORTER
Influenced by styles and technology from Germany, England and the Czech Republic, Baltic porters are a somewhat hybrid category of strong beer brewed in Slavic, Baltic and Scandinavian countries. Traditionally Baltic porters are top fermented like the porters of London, but others are bottom fermented.

Ingredients
7 lb (3.25 kg) American 2-row
1 lb (450 g) German Vienna
3 lb (1.3 kg) German Munich
1 lb (450 g) American crystal 120 L
1 lb (450 g) American chocolate
4 oz (120 g) American black patent
2 oz (56 g) Hallertauer
3.25 oz (90 g) cane sugar, for bottle
conditioning

Method

1. Step infuse by steeping all grains in with 2 quarts (2 liters) of water at 95°F (35°C) for 20 minutes.

2. Increase temperature to 122°F (50°C) for another 20 minutes.

3. Increase temperature to 158°F (70°C). As the mash reaches this temperature, remove 2 quarts (2 liters) and bring this to a strong boil for 20 minutes (this causes a caramelization, giving a fuller flavor to the beer). Return to main mash.

4. Increase temperature of mash to 167°F (75°C) for 10 minutes.

5. Sparge with 11 quarts (10 liters) of water at 167°F (75°C), collecting about 21 quarts (20 liters) of wort.

6. Add the hops to the wort and boil for 60 minutes.

7. At end of boil, remove hops and transfer to fermenting container. If necessary, top up to 20 quarts (19 liters). Pitch yeast at 70°F (21°C).

8. Ferment for 3 days and rack to secondary fermenter.

9. Ferment for 3 weeks at 61°F (16°C).

10. Bulk prime with 3.25 ounces (90 grams) of cane sugar before bottling.

AUSTRALIAN BEER

GOLDEN LAGER

Lagers are the most popular beers in Australia and are usually light-flavored and well-carbonated. They are made to be very refreshing and drinkable.

Ingredients

6 lb (2.75 kg) light malt extract
1 oz (28 g) Willamette hops
0.5 oz (14 g) Perle hops
0.5 oz (14 g) Cascade hops
1 tsp Irish moss
Lager yeast
3.5 oz (100 g) cane sugar, for bottle conditioning

Method

1. Boil 8 quarts (8 liters) of water in pot and heat to just boiling. Remove pot from heat. Add malt extract and the Willamette and Perle hops (in hop bag) and boil for 60 minutes.

2. After wort has boiled for 45 minutes, add Irish moss.

3. After wort has boiled for 58 minutes, add Cascade hops to hop bag and boil 2 more minutes.

4. Add 13 quarts (12 liters) cold water to the fermenting bucket. Strain wort into fermenter and additional cold water to make 20 quarts (19 liters).

HEDGEROW BEERS

DANDELION BEER

Dandelion beer is a classic British hedgerow
mead, flavored with dandelions. This is a
traditional recipe and was the drink of
choice for the iron workers of the Black
Country.

Ingredients

9 oz (250 g) young dandelion plants
pulled up by the roots
5 quarts (5 liters) unchlorinated water
1 in (3 cm) piece of root ginger, bruised
18 oz (500 g) honey
18 oz (500 g) demerara sugar
Juice and rind of 1 lemon
0.75 oz (25 g) cream of tartar
2 tsp yeast nutrient
Yeast (Epernay II is good but champagne
yeast would also work)

Method

1. Wash the dandelion plants and place in a
large pot along with the bruised ginger and
the lemon rind (ensure there's no pith).
Bring the mixture to the boil and allow to
simmer for 10 minutes.

2. Add the honey and sugar a little at a
time until it dissolves then turn off the
heat, add the yeast nutrient and allow to
cool slightly before straining. Add the
lemon juice and when the mixture reaches
about 99°F (37°C), add the yeast.

3. Now follow the instructions for the Basic
Mead recipe on pages 120–121.

————————

NETTLE BEER

This is an easy recipe to follow and creates a
delightful, if unusual, tasting beer. It is very
cheap to make and follows a traditional
English recipe. Before hops were widely
used in the 17th century, all sorts of plants
were used to flavor the ale including nettles
(*Urtica dioica*). It was also thought to help
alleviate rheumatic pain, gout and asthma.

Ingredients

- 2 lb (900 g) young nettle tops
- 5 quarts (5 liters) water
- 0.5 lb (230 g) sugar, brown or demerara
- 0.3 oz (7.5 g) fresh yeast
- Small piece of toast
- 0.3 oz (7.5 g) ground ginger

Method

1. Boil the nettle tops in the water for 30 minutes (you will need a very large pot for this or, preferably, a cauldron).

2. Strain the mixture and add sugar, stirring to dissolve. Add the ginger.

3. Pour mixture into a sterile container, such as a brewer's bucket.

4. Spread the yeast onto the toast and float on the surface of the nettle liquid. Cover and leave for about 3 days at room temperature. Do not allow the temperature to fluctuate too much as this will ruin the fermentation process.

5. Strain again and put into clean, strong screwtop beer bottles, or sealable wine bottles. This can be drunk after about 2 days, but does improve with maturing.

———••=•••••——

HERB BEER

Herb beer is a classic British wild country beer made with a combination of nettles and dandelion flowers. It is an excellent springtime fermented drink, made when the nettles and dandelion flowers are young and tender.

Ingredients

- 1 handful young nettle tops
- 1 handful dandelion flowers
- 23.75 oz (675 g) sugar
- 2 Tbsp freshly-grated ginger
- 2 lemons, sliced
- 1 oz (15 g) yeast

Method

1. Add the nettles to a pot. Cover with 5 quarts (5 liters) of water, bring to the boil and cook for 10 minutes. Strain into a bowl and set aside.

2. Meanwhile, add the dandelion flowers to a pot, cover with 5 quarts (4.5 liters) of water and boil for 10 minutes before straining into the bowl with the nettle liquid.

3. Stir in the sugar and ginger and mix well to combine.

4. Transfer to a fermenting bucket, arrange the lemon slices on top and scatter the yeast over everything. Cover and allow to stand overnight then strain the liquid, bottle it and store in a cool, dark place for a minimum of 3 weeks before consuming.

———••=•••••——

DANDELION AND BURDOCK BEER

Dandelion and burdock beer is a traditional British country beer made from water infused with a flavoring (dandelion and burdock roots). Though this is traditionally classed as a beer, its character is more that of a sparkling wine.

Ingredients

4 large burdock roots
3 large dandelion roots
4 quarts (4 liters) water
3 oranges, cut into segments (with peel)
3 lemons, cut into segments (with peel)
2 lb (900 g) sugar cubes

Method

1. Only collect burdock roots just as the leaves begin to emerge. Clean the roots thoroughly then chop into small pieces. (Note that dandelion roots are very bitter, so always add more burdock root than dandelion root)

2. Add 4 quarts (4 liters) of water, bring to the boil and allow to boil rapidly for 20 minutes. Add the sugar and fruit and continue boiling for 10 minutes, then remove from the heat.

3. Pour through a sieve into a fermenting bucket and allow to cool to 99°F (37°C).

4. Spread a piece of toast with 0.5 oz (15 g) yeast and float this on the surface of the liquid. Allow to ferment for 3 days then rack into bottles (flip-top bottles are best). Stopper the bottles securely then lay down in a cool place. The beer will be ready to drink in 2 months.

ELDERFLOWER BEER

This is another traditional British country beer made from water infused with elderflowers.

Ingredients

2 quarts (2 liters) elderflowers
4 quarts (4 liters) water
3 oranges, cut into segments (with peel)
3 lemons, cut into segments (with peel)
2 lb (900 g) sugar cubes
Piece of rye bread

Method

1. Combine the water, oranges, lemons and sugar in a large pot. Bring to the boil and cook for 30 minutes. Take off the heat and add the elderflowers. Set aside to infuse for 2 hours then pour through a sieve.

2. Return the liquid to a pot and heat to 99°F (37°C) before pouring into a fermenting bucket. In this case, there should be enough natural yeast in the elderflowers to begin fermentation, but if you want to be sure add a piece of rye bread to the mixture.

3. Allow to ferment for 3 days then rack

into bottles (flip-top bottles are best). Stopper the bottles securely then lay down in a cool place. The beer will be ready to drink in 2 months.

HEATHER ALE

Heather ale is a classic Scottish ale, that is designed to have a high alcohol content and is flavored with heather tips.

Ingredients

5.5 lb (2.5 kg) milled pale malted barley
9 oz (250 g) milled crystal malt
Cold water
8 large handfuls heather flowers
2 handfuls bog myrtle leaves
2 tsp baker's or beer yeast
1 level tsp sugar or honey per 25 fl oz (750 ml) bottle

Method

1. Put the milled pale malted barley and crystal malt into a 15-quart (14-liter) preserving pan. Mix with cold water, then add more water to cover grain. Stir into a slack, sloppy mixture.

2. Heat very slowly, over 3 hours, until warm. Do not allow the temperature to go above 158°F (70°C). If it gets too hot, remove from the heat and mix until it cools down. Mix every half hour.

3. Peg a coarse dishcloth or muslin over a second pot or bucket and strain the liquor. Rinse the grains with several kettles of hot water and leave to drain. Boil this liquid for 1 hour with five handfuls of heather flowers and one handful of bog myrtle leaves.

4. Rinse the dishcloth and peg over the fermentation bucket. Place three handfuls of heather and one of bog myrtle in the cloth and then pour the hot liquor over this into the bucket. Make up the bucket to 15 quarts (14 liters) with cold water and leave to cool to body temperature.

5. Add 2 teaspoons of baker's yeast or a sachet of beer yeast and leave for 6 to 8 days to ferment. Adding more wild heather flowers will ferment the ale but the flavor will be more sour and wine-like.

6. Once the ale has stopped fizzing, pour it into strong, screwtop lemonade or beer bottles (25 fl oz, 750 ml). Add 1 level teaspoon of sugar or honey to each bottle, replace top and store in a cool place until clear.

SPRUCE BEER

Spruce beer is a classic ancient hedgerow beer flavored with spruce twigs. Pick only the fresh-growing tips of spruce trees (May or June is the best time).

Ingredients

    24 quarts (23 liters) of water
    2 oz (56 g) hops
    14 oz (15 g) dried, bruised ginger root
    18 oz (500 g) of the outer twigs of
        spruce fir
    4 quarts (4 liters) molasses
    Yeast

Method

1. In a large preserving pan, combine the water, hops, ginger root and spruce fir twigs. Boil together until all the hops sink to the bottom of the pan.

2. Strain into a large crock and stir in the molasses. After this has cooled, add the yeast. Cover and leave to set for 48 hours.

3. Then bottle, cap and leave in a warm place (70 to 75°F, 21 to 24°C) for 5 days. It will now be ready to drink. Store upright in a cool place.

You can use any treacle from light to dark instead of the molasses. Dark treacle gives a very dark beer but the flavor of the treacle tends to dominate that of the finished product. You can also add other flavorings and spices such as horseradish (which is the Russian version of this beer).

ALCOHOLIC GINGER BEER

Ginger beer was one of the most popular beverages in both America, Canada and Europe until 1919 (Prohibition) in America and the 1950s in Europe. There are two ways of making ginger beer. The first consists of shredding ginger root and boiling it up with water and sugar. The second involves making a ginger "plant," which can be re-used time and time again. This makes a batch once a week. The brewing process that will be discussed in this entry is the latter.

Equipment

    A jar and lid that is big enough to
        contain the plant
    1 20-fl-oz (591-ml) measuring jug
    Several clean and dry 2-quart (2-liter)
        plastic bottles
    Teaspoons
    A large pot
    A fine cloth for straining the plant

Ingredients

    Dried ginger
    Dried yeast
    Sugar
    Juice of 4 lemons
    Water

Making the Plant

The plant is a mixture of dried ginger, yeast, sugar and water, which creates a yeast culture.

1. In the jar, place 1 teaspoon of dried yeast, 2 teaspoons of dried ginger, 4 teaspoons of sugar and 20 fl oz (591 ml) of cold water. Stir and keep at room temperature.

2. Feed the plant every day with 2 teaspoons of dried ginger and 4 teaspoons of sugar. Stir after feeding.

3. The plant will be ready after 1 week.

Making the Ginger beer
1. Place 2 lb (1 kg) of sugar and 1 quart (1 liter) of boiling water in the large pot. The sugar will dissolve.

2. Add the juice of the 4 lemons to the pan.

3. Strain the contents of the jar – the plant – through the cloth into the pan. *See below for what is to be done with the solid portion of the plant.*

4. Add 6.6 liters of room-temperature water.

5. Stir and bottle. Fill the bottles about seven-eighths full as you need to allow for expansion. Squeeze the air out of the bottles to stop them exploding under pressure from their contents.

6. Store the bottles in a safe place at room temperature, and leave for three to four weeks to 'brew'.

7. Discard half of the solid from the plant or give it to someone so they may start their own. Place the remaining half in a clean jar with a pint of water and continue to feed as above.

Wine

MAKING WINE AT HOME

Making wine at home is a great way to understand what makes a wine and how many, very subtle factors affect a wine's flavor, aroma and bouquet. Don't constrain yourself to just making wine from grapes, you can make a brilliant country wine from hedgerow ingredients, comparable with the best grape wine.

Archaeologists believe wine originated in the Near East, in the area now known as Georgia and Iran, around 6000 to 5000 BC. The nearby empires of Sumer and Egypt around 3000 BC also grew grapes for winemaking. Wine existed in ancient Greece and was an intrinsic part of its culture. Rituals celebrating Dionysus, the Greek god of wine, unsurprisingly involved drunken revelry.

The Romans adopted many aspects of Greek culture, not least the love of wine. With the growth of the Roman Empire, the production of wine spread throughout Europe wherever the climate was suitable.

The Roman Catholic Church, which uses wine as an integral part of the sacrament of Mass, was probably the cause for the drink to be brought to the Americas, following their discovery in the 15th century.

Many people, when they think of winemaking, think of grapes. The grape has been universally accepted as the most reliable fruit for winemaking, but great wines can be made from fruits other than grapes. The range of ingredients used for country winemaking is wide and varied. Country wines are fermented from the juices of fruits, vegetables or flowers and usually made in late summer and autumn when the fruits are more plentiful. Often it is a surplus of fruit or vegetables that motivates people into winemaking.

Like grape wines, good country wines take at least 6 to 18 months to mature but they are well worth the wait and each country wine will have its own distinctive qualities.

WINE FROM GRAPES

Making wine from fresh grapes can be a complex process, but also very rewarding and satisfying. Many home winemakers start with concentrate-based kits and eventually graduate to fresh grapes in order to improve their skills and the quality of their wines.

MAKING RED OR WHITE WINES

There is one major difference in the making of red and white wines. For white wines all the grape skins are removed from the juice before fermentation. For red wines the skins and seeds are fermented along with the pulp and juice for the first days of fermentation.

To make red wine, the grape pulp, the skins and the seeds are fermented together for several days, and then after most of the sugar has been fermented a winepress is used to separate the liquid from the solid materials. Only red grapes are used to make red wine.

To make white wine the grapes are crushed and then pressed to separate the juice from the solids. The resulting juice is then clarified before being fermented. White or red grapes can be used to make white wine. The juice of red wine grapes is colorless—it is the grape skins that provide the color of red wine.

FERMENTATION

The main aim of the fermentation process in making wine is the conversion of the two major grape sugars (glucose and fructose) into alcohol. This is called primary fermentation.

In the making of most red wines and some white wines, a conversion of malic acid into lactic acid also takes place in a secondary fermentation.

Other fermentations can also take place but are unwanted. For example, some bacteria can produce acetic acid (vinegar) from the grape sugars or alcohol.

It is important that the winemaker control the fermentation process and only let the required conversions take place. This is done by cleaning and sanitizing all equipment and adding crushed campden tablets to the freshly made juice to kill off any unwanted yeast and bacteria before the wine yeast is added.

STABILIZATION

Crushed campden tablets are added at the end of fermentation to ensure the process comes to a halt. This is usually done in order to make sure fermentation does not continue in the bottle and pop the cork or cause the bottle to explode.

Another reason to stop a fermentation is to produce a sweet wine i.e. one with a bit of residual sugar left in it.

Campden tablets work better when used in conjuction with potassium sorbate, which stops the yeast from reproducing.

To stabilize 5 quarts (5 liters) of wine, take 1 quart (1 liter) of the wine, add 1/2 teaspoon of potassium sorbate and 2 crushed campden tablets, stir until fully dissolved and return the rest of the wine.

CLARIFICATION

After fermentation, the wine will have an opaque, cloudy appearance due to the dead yeast cells, crystals and particles of grape tissue being held in suspension. Most of this detritus will settle naturally as sediment, given time, but the smaller particles may not. These particles can be filtered out of the wine and this is done mainly by commercial winemakers. Most home winemakers use finings, which bind with these particles and help them drop out of solution.

A fining agent is usually added to a wine after the fermentation has ended to accelerate the fall-out of yeast cells and to reduce any visible hazes that may be lingering. Finings can also be added to a wine a few days before bottling.

Finings can be added more than once if necessary. For example, a fining agent can be used to help the yeast cells drop out quickly after fermentation and then a different fining can be used before bottling to help lighten the wine's color.

Commonly used finings include:

Bentonite

A fine clay powder that can be used to clear any wine. It forms a gelatinous paste that causes the proteins to coagulate and sink to the bottom leaving a clear wine. It aids the removal of yeast cells and excessive tannin making the wine more stable in warmer storage temperatures. Unlike many other finings, it is suitable for vegetarians.

Gelatin

Gelatin needs sufficient tannin to be present in the wine for it to settle out completely and is therefore used mainly in red wines. Can be used in white wines if tannin is added at the same time.

Isinglass

This fining agent is used to give a final polish to a wine, not to remove a heavy cloudiness. It is therefore used mainly just before the bottling stage.

WINE AGING

A good wine needs an appropriate amount of time to develop just as much as it requires quality ingredients. Wine can be aged in a bottle but it is better to "bulk age" red wine for a period of time before bottling. Bulk aging is done by storing the whole batch of wine together in the same container for around 3 to 6 months. Wineries often use oak barrels to age wine but for most home winemakers the best option is to use a 24 quart (23 liter) glass carboy with oak chippings added, if required. It is not worth bulk aging quantities of less than 24 quarts (23 liters).

The aging process improves the flavor of the wine, and for a red wine it can also improve the body. The most significant improvement to all wine styles is given to the bouquet.

The formation of a wine bouquet is a result of the winemaking process. The ingredients, yeast, bacteria and winemaking procedures all produce some part of a wine's bouquet. Some of the bouquet is there soon after the completion of fermentation, but some of these components fade with time. On the other hand, some of the bouquet may require several years to develop fully. For example the fresh, fruity nose so typical of a Riesling is short-lived and therefore it is best consumed when young. A complex red, on the other hand, will need time for the wine acids to react with alcohols to produce volatile esters. A red wine also needs time to allow oxidation to subtly influence changes to the wine's ingredients.

After the wine is bottled, oxygen is no longer available, and a different type of aging begins to take place. The aroma of the wine, which is given by the variety of grape, decreases in influence and as this happens the bouquet increases.

To bulk age 24 quarts (23 liters) of red wine when the fermentation has finished:

1. Do not use finings but give the fermenter a good swirl round to bring the yeast back into suspension. Let it sit in the same conditions as during fermentation with the airlock still in place for another 4 weeks.

2. After the 4 weeks, rack the wine off the sediment and into the primary fermenter. Add 1 heaping teaspoon of sodium metabisulfite. Stir the wine well for 5 to 10 minutes to de-gas the liquid and dissolve the metabisulfite.

3. Transfer the wine into a 24-quart (23-liter) glass carboy. Fill the carboy to a level 2 in (5 cm) from the bottom of the stopper. Top up with a red wine of a similar style if need be. Add oak chippings now if desired.

4. After 3 months, rack the wine off the sediment into another carboy. Taste wine to determine whether to carry on with addition of oak chippings. Add oak if required and top up with a suitable red wine. Repeat this process every 3 months up to a total of a year.

5. Add finings if required before bottling. Add 1/8 teaspoon of metabisulfite to the 24 quarts (23 liters) if the wine is to be aged in the bottle for more than a year.

BASIC WINEMAKING

Let's assume a good season in the garden has produced a good crop of grapes. Here's everything you need to make your first batch of wine from fresh grapes. Below you'll find step-by-step recipes for a dry red and a dry white table wine. The recipes have similar steps and techniques, with one important difference. Red wines are always fermented with the skins and pulp in the fermenting vessel; the solids are pressed after fermentation is complete. White wines are pressed before fermentation, so only the grape juice is fermented.

DRY RED TABLE WINE

This will produce approx 5 quarts (5 liters).

Ingredients
    12 lb (5.5 kg) red grapes
    Pectolase
    Campden tablets
    Wine yeast
    Table sugar, if necessary

Equipment
    Large nylon straining bag
    Small food grade bucket with lid (11 to
        16 quarts, 10 to 15 liters)
    Cheesecloth
    Siphon tubing and sediment trap
    2 demijohns
    Fermentation lock and bung
    Wine bottles
    Corks
    Hand corker
    Hydrometer
    Thermometer

First and foremost, clean and sanitize all equipment.

The grapes should be ripe and taste sweet and slightly tart. If you have a hydrometer, you can ensure the grapes are ripe by squishing up a good double handful, straining the juice and measuring the sugar level. Ideally, the density should be around 1.098 specific gravity.

Place the straining bag inside the bucket and then inspect the fruit as you add it to the bag. The grapes must be clean, sound and free of insects and other debris. Remove them from the stems and while doing this discard any grapes that look rotten or otherwise suspicious. If the grapes are ripe they will crush easily by hand or you can use a potato masher. Add pectolase and 1 crushed campden tablet and stir well. Cover the bucket with cheesecloth and let sit for one hour.

Use the hydrometer to take an SG reading of the juice. You are looking for a reading of around 1.080. If you need to increase the density, make a sugar syrup by dissolving 7 ounces (200 grams) sugar into 3 fl oz (100 ml) of water. Bring it to a boil in a saucepan and immediately remove from heat. Cool before adding small amounts, 2 tablespoons at a time, until the desired specific gravity is reached. To lower the density, dilute the must with pre-boiled water.

Dissolve the yeast in 1 quart (1 liter) of warm (79° to 90°F, 26° to 32°C) water and let it stand for around 10 minutes. When it's bubbling, pour yeast solution on the must and stir gently. Cover bucket with cheesecloth and keep in a warm place (64° to 75°F, 18° to 24°C). Keep the skins under the juice at all times and mix twice daily.

Once the must has reached a density of 0.998 SG, lift the nylon straining bag out of the bucket and squeeze any remaining liquid into the bucket.

Cover the bucket and let the wine settle for 24 hours. Rack the wine off the sediment and into a sanitized demijohn, topping up with pre-boiled, cooled water to entirely fill the container. Fit with a sanitized bung and fermentation lock. Keep the container topped with grape juice or any red wine of a similar style. After 10 days, rack the wine into another sanitized demijohn. If need be, top up again with red wine of a similar style. After 6 months, siphon the cleared, settled wine off the sediment and into clean, sanitized bottles and cork. Store bottles in a cool, dark place and wait at least 6 months before drinking.

DRY WHITE TABLE WINE

This will produce about 5 quarts (5 liters).

Ingredients

12 lb (5.5 kg) white grapes
Campden tablets
Wine yeast
Table sugar, if necessary

Equipment

Large nylon straining bag
Small food grade bucket with lid (11 to 16 quarts, 10 to 15 liters)
Cheesecloth
Siphon tubing and sediment trap
2 demijohns
Fermentation lock and bung
Wine bottles
Corks
Hand corker
Hydrometer
Thermometer

Clean and sanitize all equipment.

The grapes should taste sweet, ripe and slightly tart. If you have a hydrometer, you can ensure the grapes are ripe by squishing up a good double handful, straining the juice and measuring the sugar level. Ideally, the density should be around 1.0982 specific gravity.

Place the straining bag inside the bucket and then inspect the fruit as you add it to the bag. The grapes must be clean, sound and free of insects and other debris. Remove them from the stems and while doing this discard any grapes that look rotten or otherwise suspicious. If the grapes are ripe they will crush easily by hand or you can use a potato masher. Add pectolase and 1 crushed campden tablet and stir well. Cover the bucket with cheesecloth and let sit for 1 hour.

Lift the nylon straining bag out of the bucket. Wring the bag to extract as much juice as possible. You should have about 5 quarts (5 liters) of juice in the bucket.

Use the hydrometer to take an SG reading of the juice. You are looking for a reading of around 1.080. If you need to increase the density, make a sugar syrup by dissolving 7 ounces (200 grams) sugar into 3 fl oz (100 ml) of water. Bring it to a boil in a saucepan and immediately remove from heat. Cool before adding small amounts, one tablespoon at a time, until the desired specific gravity is reached. To lower the density, dilute the must with pre-boiled water.

Allow the must to settle for 2 to 3 hours and then rack the must off the sediment and into a demijohn and add the yeast and yeast nutrient. Fit the airlock and bung. Leave in a warm place and after 10 to 14 days, when the fermentation has ceased, siphon the wine from the sediment into another demijohn, refit airlock and move to a cool place. After 2 days, siphon again and add 1/2 teaspoon of potassium sorbate and 2 crushed campden tablets.

After 3 months siphon the clarified wine off the sediment and into clean, sanitized bottles and cork them. Store the bottles in a cool, dark place and wait at least 3 months before drinking.

CLEANING AND SANITIZING

It is estimated that 90 percent of winemaking failures can be traced to poor cleaning or sanitizing. Bacteria can infect a wine and turn it bad at any stage of production if dirty equipment or bottles are used; and the wine will then be wasted.

This means that all the ingredients, utensils and equipment that come into contact with your wine at any time must first be washed or rinsed and then sterilized. This includes even small items that might be overlooked, such as spoons, straining bag, hydrometer and siphon tube. Otherwise, sooner or later, you'll produce an infected wine with a nasty taste and smell.

As well as the risk from bacteria, wild yeasts abound on fruit and in the air. Unlike cultured wine yeasts, these yeasts can only produce small amounts of alcohol; they also taint a wine with all kinds of unpleasant flavors.

WINEMAKING EQUIPMENT

FERMENTING VESSELS

Demijohn
The glass demijohn is ideal for making small batches of wine at home. It is relatively easy to clean and sanitize. For 5 quarts (5 liters) of wine it leaves just sufficient air space as it actually has a volume for nearly 5 quarts (5 liters).

Carboy
Carboys are glass containers usually of around 20 to 24 quarts (19 to 23 liters) in volume; they are good for larger fermentations.

Fermenting bucket
The fermenting bucket, as used for brewing beer at home, is good for 26-quart (25-liter) batches of wine.

Buckets
Even if the main fermenting vessel is to be a demijohn or fermenting bucket, an additional food grade buckets with lids are always useful. Country wines often need to be started in a bucket before being transferred to a demijohn. Buckets are also used for purposes such as pulping and racking off. Do not use colored buckets that may leech out dyes that may be toxic.

OTHER EQUIPMENT

Saucepan
Can be used for pre-boiling water prior to use in the winemaking process. This sterilizes and helps boil off the added chemicals and the natural limescale found in tap water. Pans or other large pots can also be used to boil fruits to extract flavors.

Do not use iron, copper or aluminum utensils as these metals react with acids in the wine. Stainless steel pots should be used.

Airlock
A simple plastic or glass device, used when fermenting a wine, prevents the outside air

from gaining access to the wine, while allowing the carbon dioxide produced during fermentation to escape. It also prevents bacteria and fruit flies from entering the wine. (Small fruit flies carry the bacteria that turn wine sour or vinegary.)

Thermometer

Ensuring the correct temperature is maintained is essential at many stages of the winemaking process.

Hydrometer

You can make wine without a hydrometer but it is an extremely useful tool. A hydrometer measures the density or specific gravity (SG) of a liquid.

In winemaking a hydrometer is also used to measure the amount of sugar in a juice or must. A reading is usually taken before fermentation so that the amount of sugar required to reach a desired final alcohol content can be calculated.

The progress of fermentation can be monitored and this allows the winemaker to determine when fermentation is finished or should be stopped. The actual percentage of alcohol can be calculated using the original and final gravity readings.

An appropriate sized trial jar is needed to hold a sample for testing. Always clean and

sanitize hydrometer, trial jar and siphon before use. Do not return samples to the must or wine.

Wine bottles

Six 25 fl oz (750 ml) bottles will store one demijohn's worth of wine. Use clear bottles for white wine, but dark bottles for red wine as it will lose its color in a clear bottle.

Corks

There are a number of different types of corks available. There are tapered corks that can be pushed in by hand, some have a plastic top for ease of extracting and others are made of plastic. When using any of these corks, store filled bottles upright.

Straight corks are best, especially for

wine of good enough quality to store and age for an amount of time. A corking tool will be needed to compress them into the bottle mouth. This ensures the correct seal for bottles to be stored in a wine rack.

There are many different grades of straight corks. Some require soaking in water to make them supple enough to go into the bottle. This soaking of corks has the risk of spoiling wine by introducing off flavors from the water on the cork. Waxed corks do not need soaking and are simpler to install.

Corking Tool

For ease of use, the two-handled corking tool is considered the best option. Leave a minimum of 0.5 in (15 mm) between the stopper and the wine, to allow room for the wine to expand with an increase in temperature.

The corked bottle should be left standing for a specified amount of time (usually a week is sufficient) to allow residual gas to escape.

Funnel

A large funnel makes it much easier to pour liquids into a demijohn. Can be used in conjunction with muslin cloth to strain juices and musts.

Filter bag

A large nylon filter bag can be used for straining fruit and flowers from wine musts. Coarse bags clog less easily than the finer bags, and are more suitable for flowers and grains.

Gloves

A pair of medium weight rubber household gloves can be useful when pulping and pressing fruit. Be sure to sanitize well before and after use.

Siphon tubing

Best when used in conjunction with a sediment trap, which shields the pipe inlet from the sediment.

Wine press

A wine press will aid in extracting the maximum amount of juice from any fruit Hard fruits such as apples will need to be pulped first.

Wine thief

This is a glass or food-grade plastic pipette used to remove an amount of wine from a demijohn or other vessel for testing.

Wine racks

A wine rack will be needed once you are hooked on winemaking. It is important you locate your rack in a suitable place. Position it where there is a constant temperature of between 48 to 60°F (9 to 15°C). Ideally it should be in a slightly humid environment to prevent the cork from drying out. Keep it out of direct sunlight, which can spoil a wine's color or create off flavors in the bottle.

CLEANING AND SANITIZING

All equipment used in the production of wine must be clean. All equipment that comes into contact with the must or wine should be sanitized. Hands should also be sanitized.

Any non-scented dishwashing detergent can be used to clean equipment as long as it is rinsed off.

To sanitize equipment you can use the following methods:

Boiling

A basic way to sanitize is to boil equipment in water. High temperatures will need to be applied over a length of time to kill off bacteria and other microorganisms. Keep equipment in water at a rolling boil for at least 15 minutes. This is, of course, unsuitable for large or delicate items.

Chlorine

Chlorine in the form of diluted bleach can be used as a cleaner and disinfectant. Bleach can taint wine and impart off flavors if not rinsed thoroughly from the equipment or if used in too strong a solution. It is usually used only as a stop gap alternative if better sanitizers are not available.

To make a sanitizing solution, mix ¼ teaspoon of unscented household bleach with 4 quarts (4 liters) of water.

Campden tablets/potassium metabisulfite

Potassium metabisulfite is the active ingredient of campden tablets. Crushed campden tablets dissolved in water make a great sanitizing solution for winemaking equipment. To make a sanitizing solution, crush 14 campden tablets and dissolve into 4 quarts (4 liters) of water.

Potassium metabisulfite is available in powder form. Dissolve 1 teaspoon of crystals in 4 quarts (4 liters) of water to make a sanitizing solution.

Campden tablets can also be used to "clean" musts before fermentation.

Propriety cleaner/sanitizers

There are many purpose-made sanitizers available using iodine, chlorine, acid or oxygen as the main active ingredient.

No rinse sanitizers are available, which save some time and remove the risk of imparting off flavors as long as they are used according to the instructions.

MAKING WINE FROM KITS

There are many winemaking kits available. They contain not only all the ingredients that are needed, but also any additives, all pre-measured. The instructions are easy to follow even for the beginner, and the results are fairly reliable. The recipes can be altered; if you want a bigger, fuller wine, add less water to the concentrate. Kits are easy to use and this makes them the best way for a beginner to learn winemaking.

You will first of all have to decide what quantity to make. Kits generally come in either 6-bottle or 30-bottle sizes.

The 6-bottle kit is a good place to start for the newcomer to winemaking. Not only do they cost less but they also involve a lot less investment in equipment. They are more convenient if you have limited space.

With 30-bottle kits, you have a bigger choice in the grape and styles offered. It doesn't take any more time to produce 30 bottles than it does 6, so a bigger kit could be a better investment in terms of the time spent. These kits come with 5 quarts (5 liters), 8 quarts (8 liters), 11 quarts (10 liters) or 16 quarts (15 liters) of concentrated grape juice, which is topped up with water (with sugar sometimes added) to make the 24 quarts (23 liters) or 30 bottles.

Many wine kits claim to be drinkable in 28 days. This might be possible but the resulting wine is likely to be worse than the nastiest plonk on a supermarket shelf.

HOW TO MAKE A YEAST STARTER

This is not the same as simply rehydrating dried yeast. In making a starter you prepare your yeast to be vigorous and strong. A starter needs to be made 2 to 3 days before the yeast is pitched.

Obtain a preservative-free grape juice (other juices can be used for country wines). If using fresh juice, boil and allow to cool before use.

For 24 quarts (23 liters) of wine, pour half a quart (0.5 liter) of juice in a sanitized jug and stir in 5 teaspoons of yeast, 1/4 teaspoon of yeast nutrient and 2 teaspoons of sugar. Cover jug and keep in a warm, dark place.

Add the starter to the wine must when it is foaming and active. When adding the starter to the must, gently swirl the sediment up off the bottom of the starter, so that the entire starter is added to the wine.

If you want to make truly drinkable wine allow it a bit of time. Give even a 28 day wine kit at least 6 months before bottling, and the resulting wine will be far superior.

If you choose to produce a 30-bottle kit, use the following schedule:

Day 1: Clean and sanitize all equipment. Rehydrate the concentrated must to the full 24 quarts (23 liters). Use pre-boiled and cooled tap water.

If you're making a full-bodied red wine, you may wish to add tannin. If so, dissolve 1 teaspoon of grape tannin in 1 quart (1 liter) of boiling water and add to a glass carboy as part of the total 24 quarts (23 liters). Draw off 4 quarts (4 liters) of the must to a jug, seal with cling film and keep in the fridge. If your kit came with oak, add it now as per instructions.

Aerate the must by stirring vigorously and then pitch the yeast. Transfer the fermenter to a warm dark place with a temperature around 68°F (20°C). Keep the fermenter covered with a clean sanitized cloth.

Day 2: After 48 hours gently stir the must and fit the lid and airlock to the bucket.

Days 3 to 5: Gently stir the must once a day.

Days 7 to 10: The fermentation should slow and calm down around this time. When it does, take the 4 quarts (4 liters) of must from the fridge and allow it to reach room temperature. When at room temperature add to the carboy slowly and stir gently. Return the carboy to the warm place.

Days 11 to 27: Keep the carboy in a warm place. Check occasionally to make sure the airlock has not emptied.

Day 28: Measure and make note of the specific gravity of the must. It should be under 0.995. Check the gravity on a daily basis from now until it remains unchanged for 2 consecutive days.

If making a white wine, make up a bentonite finings slurry following the instructions.

Day 30 onward: When the specific gravity stabilizes, add the stabilizer from the kit. Rack the must of the lees into another fermenting bucket.

Stir the wine vigorously to de-gas it. If making white wine add the bentonite slurry. If making red wine add the finings supplied following the instrutions. Top up with a suitable dry wine and refit the airlock and move the fermenter to a cool place.

After 14 days in the cool, dark place, rack off the wine into another sanitized carboy, top up with a dry wine if necessary. Refit the airlock and return the carboy to the cool, dark place for 30 days.

After the 30 days, repeat the racking off process as above and return the carboy to the same conditions for another 60 days.

After the 60 days de-gas the wine. Do this by stirring vigorously for 2 to 3 minutes so that the wine is aerated and foams. Let the wine rest for 10 minutes. Repeat the stirring and resting until the wine no longer foams when stirred.

Stir in ⅛ teaspoon of metabisufite and then rack the wine into bottles. Age the wine in the bottle for at least 3 months.

COUNTRY WINES

You are probably wondering what country wines are. These are wines made from fruits, herbs or vegetables other than grapes. No matter what your choice of ingredient, country wines are simple to make and require very little equipment. The rewards can be tremendous because the diversity of flavors is immense.

Country wine can be made with any fleshy fruit, such as peaches, plums or apricots or you can raid the garden for currants, blackberries and elderberries. Other possibilities include dandelions, rhubarb, oak leaves and so the list continues ad infinitum.

Winemaking in itself is a fairly basic process, which means it adapts well to a great variety of ingredients. Once the fundamentals have been mastered, you can have fun experimenting with a myriad of flavors.

But remember:

• Allow plenty of time for bottle ageing, because country wines can taste a little rough around the edges when young. They usually mature after about 6 to 12 months.

• Non-grape fruits are notoriously low in acids, which give wine a good flavor, so make sure your recipe calls for additional wine acid to correct this problem.

When making country wine, your aim should be to preserve the taste and flavor of the specific flower or fruit that has been collected. Having said that, you will be trying to produce a wine that tastes as close as possible to a commercial wine made from grapes.

The following fabulous collection of recipes have really authentic country flavors, and are designed to tempt you away from the standard grape. Hopefully the results will encourage you to experiment with all kinds of herbs, flowers, berries and even weeds to create your very own house wines.

Whether you are using grapes or country produce, your wine will change from year to year. It is down to the winemaker to bring out the best that the fruit has to offer, but weather and other contributory factors will change the flavor each time. By creating your own country wines you are not only making something completely individual, but you are giving it your own personal style.

APPLE WINE

This is a full-flavored wine, but make sure you take extra care with sterilization and be aware that the type of apple used will change the finished flavor dramatically.

Ingredients

    3.5 lb (1.5 kg) cooking apples
    2 lb (1 kg) granulated sugar
    5 quarts (5 liters) cold water
    2 lemons
    1 orange
    1 tsp wine yeast
    Yeast nutrient
    Pectic enzyme

Method

1. Wash and cut apple, but do not peel or core. You can mince the apple if your prefer as this will help enhance the flavor.
2. Put in a sterilized plastic bucket and pour 5 quarts (5 liters) of cold water over them.
3. Cover the bucket and leave for a week, but stir well every day with a plastic spoon.
4. After a week, strain the liquid through muslin into another sterilized bucket.

5. Add the sugar and the juice and grated rinds of the lemons and orange.
6. Add the yeast, yeast nutrient and pectic enzyme. Cover the bucket and leave for 24 hours.
7. Now strain the liquid, pressing all the liquid out, and place in a fermentation jar.
8. This can be used straight away as a non-alcoholic drink or left for 4 months to turn into a clear, delicious wine.

BEETROOT WINE

The color of this wine will be exactly that of the beetroot used, so make sure you only use good quality produce. Also, for the yeast to convert sugar into alcohol, it is essential to keep the oxygen out and so you need to make sure the container is completely airtight. Make sure your fermentation jars and bottled wines are not filled to the brim—it is advisable to leave some room. Once the wine is bottled it can be drunk straight away, as the color and taste changes with age. This particular wine is quite sweet, so feel free to make any adjustments with the quantity of sugar, but it would probably be best to wait until your first trial so you get an idea how much to change. It is certainly a brilliant winter warmer and a great alternative to port.

Ingredients

    2 lb (1 kg) beetroot
    2 lb (1 kg) sugar

1 tsp wine yeast

2 small unwaxed lemons

4 quarts (4 liters) of water

3 to 5 small sticks of cinnamon

7 cloves

½ cup warm water

Method

1. Wash the beetroots, peel off the skin and finely grate them.

2. Dissolve the yeast in lukewarm water with ½ teaspoon of sugar and leave to rise.

3. Boil 4 quarts (4 liters) of water in a clean saucepan.

4. Add the grated beetroot to the boiling water and leave it until it is cooked.

5. When the beetroot is soft, remove from the heat and allow it to cool down to lukewarm.

6. Strain through muslin into a sterilized glass container.

7. Add the sugar to the strained liquid and stir until it is dissolved using a wooden spatula or spoon.

8. Add the juice of the lemons, the dissolved yeast, cinnamon and cloves.

9. The container must be airtight and stored in a dark place for fermentation to take place—approximately 15 days. On the 4th or 5th day open the container and stir with a wooden spoon, then leave to rest until the 15th day.

10. After the fermentation process is complete, strain the liquid again to make sure there are no residues before placing it in sterilized bottles.

This wine can be stored and served at room temperature and is a wonderful accompaniment to a piece of fruit cake.

BIRCH SAP WINE

The birch has been put to many uses over the centuries—thatching, making wattles and even disciplining disobedient children. The sap of the tree has been used to make various beverages such as wine, beer, spirit and vinegar.

The best time to collect the sap is in the spring when it is rising, just before the leaves are open. The idea is to extract a gallon of sap from a hole drilled into the bark and then transfer it, via a plastic tube, into a glass bottle. A standard 5-quart (5-liter) bottle from a home winemaking shop takes a 1-inch (2.5-centimeter) cork, so use a hand drill and a 1-inch (2.5-centimeter) auger drill. Penetrate the bark by less than 0.25 in (6 mm), put the cork in and connect the tubing to the bottle through a second cork—leaving a little slot to let the air out.

Leave in place for two days. If conditions are right, you will collect 5 quarts (5 liters) of sap in your bottle. When removing the cork from the tree, remember to fill the hole with a complete cork, as this gives the tree an easier task in repairing its bark.

The sugar content is quite low—about 4 oz (115 g) to 5 quarts (5 liters)—so you can adjust the sweetening as to whether you want a dry or sweet wine.

Ingredients

   5 quarts (5 liters) sap
   7 oz (200 g) chopped raisins
   2 lb (1 kg) white sugar
   Juice of 2 lemons
   Packet of general purpose yeast

Method

1. Boil the sap as soon as possible after collecting, as it can very easily go bad.
2. Add the sugar to the boiling liquid and allow to simmer for 10 minutes.
3. Put the chopped raisins in a polythene bucket (one with a lid), pour the boiling liquid onto them and then add the lemon juice.
4. Start the yeast in a glass. Leave until the mixture cools to blood heat, then add the started yeast.
5. Leave to ferment in the covered bucket for 3 days and then strain off into a 5-quart (5-liter) jar and seal with an airlock.
6. Leave in a warm room or cupboard until the fermentation process is complete.
7. Rack off the wine into a clean jar and leave it until the sediment has settled. Alternatively, you can filter the wine through muslin to remove the sediment.
8. Bottle in clean, sterilized bottles, cork and store in a cool place.

This wine can be drunk after 1 month, but it is even better if you can wait 6 months. If you find that it is too dry at the bottling stage, you can sweeten it with a little sugar syrup before bottling, but be careful not to make it too sweet.

BLACKCURRANT WINE

Blackcurrants have a tough skin and they will need to be crushed, heated or broken down with a food processor in order to extract their powerful juice.

Ingredients

   3 lb (1.3 kg) ripe blackcurrants
   3 lb (1.3 kg) white sugar
   1 tsp citric acid
   5 quarts (5 liters) water
   Yeast nutrient
   1 tsp wine yeast

Method

1. Crush the blackcurrants and place in a fermentation bucket.
2. Boil the sugar in the water and pour all the liquid over the blackcurrants.
3. When it is cool, add the citric acid, yeast nutrient and wine yeast.
4. Cover and leave to ferment for 5 days, stirring daily.
5. Using a fine sieve or muslin, strain the liquid into a demijohn and fit an airlock to seal the jar.
6. Store in a warm place and allow the fermentation to work.
7. When the fermentation has ceased, rack the wine into a clean jar and place in a cooler environment. Leave alone for a few months.
8. When the wine is clear and stable, siphon into sterilized bottles. This wine can be drunk after 1 year, but it certainly improves with age.

BLACKBERRY WINE

This wine is full-bodied and will get better with age, but generally speaking berry wine should be drunk before it is 3 years old.

Ingredients

4 lb (2 kg) blackberries, freshly picked
2 lb (1 kg) white sugar
4 quarts (4 liters) of water
Red wine yeast
Campden tablets (optional)

Method

1. Crush the berries by hand in a plastic bucket and then pour on 1 quart (1 liter) of boiled water that has cooled to room temperature. Mix it well.
2. This next step is optional. Campden tablets kill any unwanted yeast, so if you want to use one, crush the tablet and dissolve the powder in a little warm water. Mix this with the fruit.
3. Leave the mixture for a couple of hours and do not worry if bleaching takes place.
4. Take a third of the sugar and boil it for 1 minute in 2 quarts (2 liters) of water. Allow this to cool to room temperature.
5. When cool, add a packet of yeast into 4 fl oz (113 ml) of warm water. Leave it to sit for 10 minutes.
6. Pour the sugar syrup into the fruit pulp. Then add the yeast and cover the bucket with a clean cloth.
7. Leave it to sit for 7 days in a warm place.

8. Strain the pulp through fine muslin and throw the pulp on your compost. Put the strained wine into a 5 quart (5 liter) demijohn.
9. Boil another third of the sugar in 0.5 quart (0.5 liter) of water and allow it to cool. Once it is at room temperature, add it to the rest of the mixture.
10. Plug the top of the demijohn with an airlock and leave it for 10 days.
11. Siphon your wine into a spare demijohn, making sure all your equipment is sterilized first.
12. Boil the remaining third of the sugar in the remaining water and allow to cool. Add it to the wine, plug the demijohn with an airlock and leave it in a warm place until fermentation ceases.
13. Siphon into a spare demijohn, leaving the sediment behind.
14. Bottle in sterilized bottles and store at room temperature.

BLACKBERRY AND ELDERBERRY WINE

Elderberries are another common fruit that can easily be grown in the garden. Try to pick the fruit on a sunny day when it will be full of natural sweetness and remove any leaves. It produces a lovely wine with a deep, rich color. Try to keep it for about a year before drinking.

Ingredients

- 2 lb (1 kg) ripe blackberries
- 2 lb (1 kg) ripe elderberries
- 3 lb (1.3 kg) white sugar
- 1½ tsp citric acid
- 1 tsp pectic enzyme
- 1 9 oz (250 g) can of red grape concentrate
- Red wine, or general purpose yeast
- 2 campden tablets

Method

1. Remove the stems and leaves from the fruit and wash thoroughly.
2. Mash the blackberries and elderberries in a clean, plastic bucket with a potato masher and pour over 2 quarts (2 liters) of boiling water. Mix well.
3. Leave to cool to about 70°F (21°C) and then add a crushed campden tablet and stir
4. Add the pectic enzyme and citric acid, stir well and then add the yeast a day later.
5. Cover the bucket and leave to ferment for 4 to 5 days, stirring daily.
6. Strain through muslin or a sieve and add 3 lb (1.3 kg) of sugar. Stir well to dissolve the sugar and pour into a demijohn.
7. Add the red grape concentrate and make up to 5 quarts (5 liters) with more water.
8. Give the mixture a final stir, fit an airlock and leave the demijohn in a warm place (68 to 72°F, 20 to 22°C) until there are no more bubbles passing through the airlock.
9. Add another campden tablet and siphon into another demijohn. Refit the airlock securely.
10. The wine will gradually clear and after about 6 weeks it should be ready to siphon off into bottles.

CHERRY WINE

This makes a delicious, sharp, dry wine. You can make it with either the big, sweet black cherries or the much smaller, yellow ones with a red blush. The varieties can be combined in one batch if you prefer. This wine is best if you can refrain from drinking it for at least a year from the date it was started.

Ingredients

- 5 quarts (5 liters) water
- 3.5 lb (1.5 kg) sugar
- 3.5 lb (1.5 kg) cherries
- 2 lemons
- 2 tsp yeast

Method

1. Pick the cherries when really ripe and remove the stalks. If you cannot find enough cherries for your recipe, you can always add shop fruit to make up the quantity, but remember this will produce a much sweeter wine so you may need to adjust the sugar content.
2. Place in a bucket, boil three-quarters of the water and pour over the fruit.
3. When it cools, mash the fruit through with your hands.
4. Leave to stand for 3 days, then squeeze the fruit through a wine bag.
5. Make up the sugar syrup with the last

quarter of the water, then put into a demijohn to ferment.

6. Grate the lemon rind and squeeze out the juice. Make up the yeast starter and add to the wine. Seal the demijohn with a cotton wool bung and leave to stand for another 3 days.

7. Now place an airlock and allow to ferment for 3 months.

8. When fermentation ceases, siphon into clean bottles and keep for at least another 3 to 4 months before drinking.

CLOVER WINE

Red clover wine can be made with either fresh or dried clover flowers. Pick the clover flowers early in the morning, but after any dew has evaporated. After picking remove the stems and wash the flowerheads well. You can pick more flowers than needed and dry them for future use if you wish. Leave this wine for at least 6 months before tasting.

Drying flowerheads

Lay the flowers on a baking tray and place them in your oven on the lowest possible setting, turning every 2 to 3 hours until absolutely dry. Place the dried flowers in sealed plastic bags for later use.

Ingredients

2 quarts (2 liters) red clover flowers
0.5 quart (0.5 liter) white grape juice
(reconstituted from concentrate)

2 lb (1 kg) white sugar
2 tsp acid blend
1 tsp yeast nutrient
¼ tsp tannin
5 quarts (5 liters) water
Wine yeast

Method

1. Remove stems from the clover flowers and wash thoroughly.

2. Place in primary fermenter and pour some boiling water over the flowers.

3. Add grape juice, acid blend, tannin, yeast nutrient and water to bring it up to 5 quarts (5 liters) in total.

4. When lukewarm, add the yeast. Cover and leave to ferment.

5. After 7 days, strain the liquid into a secondary demijohn and fit an airlock.

6. Siphon off after 60 days, top up, refit the airlock and leave for 4 months.

7. Once the bubbles have ceased in the airlock, the wine shold be clear.

8. Stabilize, wait 10 days, sweeten to taste and bottle.

COLTSFOOT WINE

Coltsfoot (*Tussilago farfara L.*) is a perennial herb found especially on waste places, gravel pits, banks and also on dunes and screes. It flowers from March to April, just before the leaves

appear. Dried leaves of coltsfoot were originally smoked as a remedy for asthma and coughs.

Traditionally, coltsfoot wine was made from the petals only, but the wine will not be affected if you leave some of the outer green calyx and stem attached.

Ingredients

- 3 quarts (3 liters) coltsfoot flowers
- 2 lb (1 kg) white sugar
- 5 quarts (5 liters) water
- Juice of 2 lemons
- Wine yeast

Method

1. Prepare the coltsfoot flowers and place them in a plastic bucket. Pour on 2 quarts (2 liters) of boiling water and leave them to soak for 24 hours, pressing occasionally with a wooden spoon.
2. Strain off the flowers through muslin, squeezing hard at the end to extract all the flavor.
3. Add the lemon juice and put the yeast to start.
4. Boil the sugar in 2 quarts (2 liters) of water to dissolve it and add to the bucket. When the liquid has cooled, add the yeast, cover and leave to ferment for 3 days.
5. Transfer the liquid to a fermentation jar. Make up the quantity with the remainder of the cold water and seal it with an airlock.
Leave in a warm place (61 to 68°F, 16 to 20°C) until fermentation has ceased.

6. Siphon off the wine into a clean demijohn, leaving the sediment behind. Seal with a cork and leave for a month.
7. Filter the wine to get a sparkling result. Bottle and cork with sterilized corks.

GORSE FLOWER WINE

Gorse (*Ulex europaeus*) is generally distributed throughout the British Isles. It occurs in rough, grassy places and on the edges of heaths. It flowers from March to June. Gorse flowers produce one of the best wines, but in ancient times they were used to flavor whisky. Make sure you pick nice fresh flowers that have come out fully. Thick gardening gloves will help to protect the wear and tear on your fingers.

Ingredients

- 2 quarts (2 liters) gorse flowers
- 2 lb (1 kg) white sugar
- 5 quarts (5 liters) water
- 2 lemons
- 2 oranges
- 5 quarts (5 liters) water
- Wine yeast

Method

1. Start the yeast.
2. Simmer the flowers in the water for 15 minutes and then dissolve the sugar. Pour into a bucket and add the juice of the oranges and lemons, plus the thinly peeled rind.

COURGETTE WINE
Although you might think this is a strange choice of vegetable to make wine, the following recipe is great if you have a glut during the season. The alcohol content reaches 10 percent, so it is not for the faint-hearted!

Ingredients
6 to 8 courgettes
Juice of 2 lemons
Juice of 1 orange
6 oz (170 g) chopped raisins
1 oz (28 g) root ginger
2 lb (907 g) sugar
5 quarts (5 liters) water
Yeast nutrient
Wine yeast

3. Allow the mixture to cool to 99°F (37°C), add the yeast and leave to stand with a cloth over it for 3 days.
4. Strain off the solids and pour into a fermentation jar. Fit an airlock and leave it to ferment.
5. When fermentation is complete, rack off into a clean jar making it up to the full amount with cold boiled water. Leave for a month and then filter, and bottle in sterilized bottles.

Method
1. Mash the courgettes, including skin and seeds, together. Add the ginger and raisins.
2. Pour on boiling water, stir thoroughly, and, when cool, add the juice from the lemons and orange, the yeast nutrient and the wine yeast.
3. Leave the pulp to ferment for 4 days, pressing down the cap twice daily, and then strain.
4. Stir in the sugar and refit the airlock, continuing the fermentation until the bubbles cease.
5. Siphon off into sterilized bottles.

Variation
An interesting variation on this wine is the addition of 1.75 oz (50 g) of root ginger. Add this to the flowers at the simmering stage.

CRAB APPLE WINE

There are two popular species of crab apples include: *Malus sylvestris*, which is a little, round apple ending up a pure yellow color when ripe; and the sub-species *malus sylvestris mitis*, which is usually bigger and more apple-shaped. The sourness of the crab apple gives rise to the expression "crabby," meaning an ill-tempered person.

Crab apples have long been used in making drinks, from cider to mead and the wassail bowl. This fruit also makes an excellent wine, well worth the effort of preparation, which has been enhanced by the flavor of cooking apples. Pick the crab apples when they are really ripe.

Ingredients

2 lb (1 kg) crab apples
3 lb (1.3 kg) sugar
2 quarts (2 liters) boiling water
0.5 lb (225 g) cooking apples
1 lemon
1 orange
Wine yeast

Method

1. Grate all the apples into a plastic bucket, using only a stainless steel grater. Alternatively, you can crush them if you find it easier.
2. Pour on the boiling water and leave to cool. Mash with the hand and leave to stand for 3 days, stirring daily.
3. Strain through a wine bag into a 5-quart (5-liter) demijohn.
4. Make up sugar syrup with 1 quart (1 liter) of water and 3 lb (1.3 kg) of sugar and pour into the wine jar. Grate orange and lemon rind and squeeze juice into the jar.
5. Prepare yeast and allow to ferment, then put into the wine jar. Make up the liquid with boiled, cooled water to the correct amount (5 quarts, 5 liters).
6. Leave wine to ferment for 4 months, then siphon into a clean 5-quart (5-liter) jar and leave for a further 3 months.

Variation

Another excellent wine can be made with 2 lb (1 kg) of crab apples and 1 lb (450 g) of blackberries, using the same method as previously stated.

DAMSON WINE

Damson wine is possibly one of the finest red country wines to make. The pectin in damsons is not easy to clear so you will need a pectin-destroying agent. However, this should produce a red wine of character especially if left to age for about a year. The result is a wonderful full-bodied wine, which tastes very similar to a Shiraz.

Ingredients

3 lb (1.3 kg) damson plums
3 lb (1.3 kg) sugar
5 quarts (5 liters) water
Citric acid
Wine yeast

Yeast nutrients

Campden tablets

Pectin-destroying enzyme

Method

1. Wash the fruit and drain it. Put the fruit in a bucket and pour over 1 quart (1 liter) of boiling water.

NOTE: Do not boil the damsons as this releases too much pectin.

2. Add 1 lb (450 g) of the sugar and citric acid, stir until the sugar has dissolved and break up the fruit with a large spoon.
3. Add a further 2 quarts (2 liters) of warm water, then add the pectin-destroying enzyme. Cover the bucket and stand it in a warm place, stirring daily.
4. After 2 days, strain it into a fermentation jar, then dissolve 1 lb (450 g) of sugar in hot water and add to the vessel.
5. Add the yeast and nutrients, then make up to 5 quarts (5 liters) with warm water. Seal the jar with an airlock.
6. When fermentation is complete, siphon into a clean container, add 1 crushed campden tablet and close the container with a bung or safely lock.
7. Rack every 2 months until it is clear in appearance.

You will de able to drink this wine in 6 months or perhaps before that, but the longer you keep it the better it will be.

DANDELION WINE

Dandelion (*Taraxacum officinale*) is a perennial herb, abundant throughout the the British Isles. It can be found in pastures, meadows, lawns, roadsides and waste places. The dandelion flowers profusely in April and the leaves can be found at any time of the year, except in the very coldest months. Pick the dandelion flowers on a sunny day, trying not to pick any of the stalk. The stalk contains a bitter milk, which could find its way into your wine and contaminate the flavor. Dandelion wine can have a rather resinous flavor, but it is a taste that gradually grows on you.

Ingredients (DRY)

3 quarts (3 liters)
    dandelion petals
1 lb (450 g) sultanas
24 oz (675 g) sugar
9.5 fl oz (280 ml) freshly made strong tea
1 tsp citric acid
2 oranges
Good wine yeast and nutrient
Few drops of pectic enzyme
Water (as in method)

Ingredients (MEDIUM)

3 quarts (3 liters) dandelion petals

1 lb (450 g) sultanas

2 lb (1 kg) sugar

9.5 fl oz (280 ml) freshly made strong tea

1 tsp citric acid

2 oranges

Good wine yeast and nutrient

Few drops of pectic enzyme

Water (as in method)

Ingredients (SWEET)

4 quarts (4 liters) dandelion petals

1 lb (450 g) sultanas

0.4 oz (1 g) sugar

9.5 fl oz (280 ml) freshly made strong tea

1 tsp citric acid

2 oranges

Good wine yeast and nutrient

Few drops of pectic enzyme

Water (as in method)

Method for all three

1. Put the flowers in the fermenting vessel with the chopped sultanas, tea, sugar and citric acid. Pour on about 4 quarts (4 liters) of boiling water. Stir well to dissolve the sugar. Cover and leave to cool to about 64°F, 18°C (lukewarm).

2. Stir in the yeast nutrient and pectic enzyme. Grate the orange rind over the mixture. Then halve the oranges and press out the juice, strain it and stir into the mixture. Cover with polythene or a fitted lid, tie down tightly with string and put the mixture in a warm place to ferment for 8 or 9 days, stirring daily.

3. Strain the solids through 3 or 4 thicknesses of muslin and press as much juice out as possible.

4. Clean the fermenting bucket and return the strained wine to this. Cover as before and leave in the warm to continue to ferment for a further 5 or 6 days, or a little longer if fermentation still appears fairly vigorous.

5. Pour carefully into a 5-quart (5-liter) jar leaving as much residue behind as possible.

6. Fill the jar to where the neck begins. If not filled to this level, top up with boiled, cooled water. Fit a fermentation lock and leave until all fermentation has ceased, before siphoning into sterilized bottles.

Keep this wine for as long as possible as it improves with age.

———

ELDERFLOWER SPARKLING WINE

Elderflowers have been used for centuries in different areas for a variety of different purposes. Bunches were hung indoors to keep flies away, blossoms were beaten into the batter of flannel cakes and muffins and in Victorian times no household would be without a bottle of elderflower water for the removal of freckles and treatment of sunburn.

This recipe makes a really refreshing summer drink, which should be served chilled with ice and lemon.

Ingredients

4 elderflower heads in full bloom
4 quarts (5 liters) cold water
1 lemon
23 oz (650 g) loaf sugar
2 Tbsp white vinegar

Method

1. Dissolve the sugar in a little warm water and leave to cool.
2. Squeeze the juice from the lemon, cut the rind in four, and put the pieces with the elderflowers in a large jug or basin. Add the wine vinegar and pour on the rest of the cold water. Leave to steep for 4 days.
3. Strain off through muslin and bottle in screwtop bottles.

This drink should be ready to drink in 6 to 10 days, but test after 6 days anyway to see that it does not get too fizzy. If it fails to work, leave it for another week. Sometimes the natural yeast of the flowers is very slow to activate and occasionally you can get a batch that fails completely.

――――●●●●――――

ELDERFLOWER WINE

Elderflower wine has a light and crisp taste with citrus notes, and is light yellow in color. There are many variations on this classic British country wine, but the main ingredients are essentially the same. The drink itself is one of the easiest wines to start with, and the key to its success is the right amount of flowers. Too many and the final product will have a rather stewed taste.

Ingredients

20 fl oz (591 ml) elderflower petals
9 oz (250 g) raisins, chopped
5 quarts (5 liters) water
2 lemons
1 campden tablet
3.5 lb (1.5 kg) sugar
1 tsp wine tannin
Packet of wine yeast and yeast nutrient

Method

1. Gather the elderflowers on a sunny day when you can smell the distinctive aroma of the flowers. Separate the flowers from the stalks by pulling through your fingers, or cutting with scissors.
2. Press the flowers down lightly into a plastic bucket.
3. Prepare the chopped raisins and the rind from the lemons (no white pith).

4. Add these to the petals in the bucket and pour over 5 quarts (5 liters) of boiling water. Allow to cool and add 1 campden tablet, crushed. Cover with a clean cloth and leave to stand for 3 days, stirring daily.

5. Add the sugar and juice from the 2 lemons, the wine tannin, yeast and yeast nutrient. Make sure all the sugar is dissolved.

6. Strain through muslin or a fine mesh bag into a 5-quart (5-liter) fermenting demijohn. Fit an airlock and leave in a warm place (about 68 to 72°F, 20 to 22°C) for about 5 days.

7. Siphon off the liquid into another clean demijohn and leave until the fermentation is complete. This will be when the bubbles no longer appear in the airlock.

8. The wine will gradually become clear and after about 8 weeks should be ready. Add another crushed campden tablet and then after 24 hours siphon into sterilized bottles.

The result is a distinctive bouquet with an exceptionally clean taste.

FIG WINE

This recipe can be made with either fresh or dried figs, and takes about 2 to 3 months to ferment. Figs make a wine of rich amber shades and whisky, caramel and tobacco flavors. It is the perfect accompaniment to a Mediterranean-style meal and will be a unique talking point at your dinner party.

Ingredients

2 lb (1 kg) dried figs
2 lb (1 kg) sugar
1 tsp pectic enzyme
9.5 fl oz (280 ml) honey
Juice of 1 lemon
Juice of 1 orange
Wine yeast
1 tsp yeast nutrient
5 quarts (5 liters) water
1 campden tablet

Method

1. Boil the water and add honey, stirring until it has completely dissolved. Simmer and remove any floating scum. Add to a fermentation vessel and allow honey mixture to cool.

2. Roughly chop the dried figs and add to 1 quart (1 liter) of boiling water. Leave the liquid to cool down for approximately 12 hours.

3. Strain the fig mixture and combine with the honey water in the fermentation vessel. Add all of the remaining ingredients, including the activated wine yeast. Stir each morning and evening for around 4 days.

4. Strain the mixture into a demijohn and attach an airlock.

5. Siphon off in about 6 weeks and then three more times at regular intervals until it is 1 year old.

6. Bottle and allow to stand for 1 year before drinking.

A sweeter version of this wine can be achieved by adding extra sugar at the first racking. Fresh figs can also be used, although the quantity should be increased to around 6 lb (2.75 kg) for this recipe.

GOOSEBERRY WINE

Gooseberry wine has a delicious, fresh fruit flavor, which is great to drink in the middle of summer and as an accompaniment to spicy food.

Ingredients

5 lb (2.25 kg) gooseberries
½ tsp pectic enzyme
½ tsp potassium sorbate
3 lb (1.3 kg) sugar
5 quarts (5 liters) water
1 tsp yeast nutrient
1 packet wine yeast
1 campden tablet

Method

1. Rinse the fruit and remove any stalks and leaves, making sure there are no rotting fruits. Add to a large pot and mash gently with a spoon to break the skins.
2. Pour boiling water over the mashed pulp. Add all the ingredients, except the yeast and potassium sorbate. Stir thoroughly, then cover and leave for 24 hours.
3. Stir again and add the yeast. Now leave for 5 to 6 days.
4. Strain the mixture through muslin or a fine sieve (pressing the pulp to extract all the mixture). Alternatively put in straining bags and squeeze tightly.
5. Pour into a sterile demijohn and fit an airlock.
6. Leave to ferment for 3 to 4 weeks (the time will depend on the temperature of the room).
7. Siphon off the wine and throw away the sediment.
8. Leave for 2 months and then re-siphon. Repeat this step twice more.
9. Add the potassium sorbate to your wine and decant into bottles. Try and leave for at least 6 months before drinking.

GREEN TOMATO WINE

Green tomato wine has a unique taste and, if it is well made, it is very enjoyable.

Ingredients

3.5 lb (1.5 kg) green tomatoes
2 lb (1 kg) sugar
1 tsp yeast nutrient
4 lemons, juice only

1 campden tablet
½ tsp pectic enzyme
2 lb (1 kg) raisins
0.5 oz (14 g) fresh ginger root
1 packet wine yeast
5 quarts (5 liters) water

Method

1. Wash and trim the tomatoes. Chop and place in a primary fermenter. Add water to make up 5 quarts (5 liters). Add all the other ingredients with the exception of the yeast. Stir well to dissolve the sugar and allow to sit overnight.

2. Sprinkle the yeast over the mixture and stir. Stir daily for 5 to 6 days, until the specific gravity is 1.040.

3. Strain the mixture through muslin and squeeze out as much juice as you can from the fruit. Siphon into a secondary fermenter and fit an airlock.

4. For a dry wine, siphon in 3 weeks and every 3 months for 1 year. Bottle.

5. For a sweet wine, siphon at 3 weeks. Add ½ cup of sugar dissolved in 1 cup of wine. Stir gently, and place back into the secondary fermenter. Repeat the process every 6 weeks until fermentation does not restart with the addition of sugar. Siphon every 3 months until it is 1 year old and then bottle.

HAW WINE

Haw wine is made from the berries of the hawthorn (*Crataegus monogyna*). In the 13th century the berries were eaten by Highlanders when thoroughly ripe, and in India the tree is cultivated for its fruit. The fruit ripens at the end of the September, but can be picked as late as November.

Ingredients

4 lb (2 kg) berries
1 lemon
2 oranges
2 lb (1 kg) brown or white sugar
5 quarts (5 liters) boiling water
1 packet wine yeast

Method

1. Put the berries in a large bowl and cover with boiling water. Leave to stand for a week, stirring daily.

2. Strain on to the thinly peeled rinds and juice of the oranges and lemons. Add the sugar melted in a little water, and stir.

3. When the mixture has cooled, add the yeast, cover and leave for 24 hours.

4. Transfer to a fermentation jar and leave until the process is complete.

This makes a very delicate pink wine that seems to benefit from keeping. It does, however, need the addition of pectin to keep it clear.

HEDGEROW PORT

This is a great combination of hedgerow berries that make a rich, port-style wine.

Ingredients

2 lb (1 kg) elderberries
9 oz (250 g) blackcurrants
18 oz (500 g) blackberries
18 oz (500 g) raisins
3 lb (1.25 kg) sugar
1 tsp tartaric acid
1 tsp pectic enzyme
½ tsp port yeast and nutrient

Method

1. Rinse the berries in cold water and place them in a large, plastic container. It is essential to remove every last piece of stalk as it can impart a bitter taste to the wine.
2. Boil the water, pour it over the berries and leave to stand for 24 hours.
3. Press the mixture through a muslin cloth.
4. Put all the other ingredients, apart from the yeast and pectic enzyme, into a preserving pan and simmer gently for an hour, skimming when necessary.
5. Allow the mixture to cool and, when it is lukewarm, stir in the yeast and pectic enzyme. Transfer it into a fermentation jar, top it up, fit an airlock and leave to stand in a dark place for 2 weeks.
6. Siphon off into a clean vessel, then siphon off into clean bottles.

Leave to mature until Christmas and enjoy with your mince pies.

HONEYSUCKLE FLOWER WINE

Honeysuckle flowers will start blooming in spring once the sun gets a little warmth on them. What better way to celebrate this time of year than by making your own batch of wine with the flowers. Make sure you only use the flowers, though, as the berries are poisonous.

Ingredients

1 quart (1 liter) honeysuckle flowers
3 lb (1.3 kg) white sugar
2 oranges
0.5 lb (225 g) raisins
2 tsp acid blend
1 tsp pectic enzyme
1 tsp tannin (or cup of black tea)
1 tsp yeast nutrient
Wine yeast
5 quarts (5 liters) cooled boiled water
1 campden tablet

Method

1. Carefully wash the honeysuckle flowers in cold water and transfer to a clean, empty winemaking fermentation bucket. Add all of the cooled, boiled water and other ingredients, with the exception of the yeast.
2. Stir the wine mixture well until all of the sugar has completely dissolved. Allow to stand for 12 hours and then add the activated wine yeast.
3. Stir every morning and evening for around 4 days and then strain thoroughly. Transfer to a sterilized wine demijohn with with an airlock.

4. Siphon off the wine after about 6 weeks, by which time the fermentation will have slowed dramatically.

5. Siphon off a further two to three times over the next year until the wine is clear.

6. Bottle and drink after at least 6 months, the longer the better.

and add to the jar.

3. Add grape juice concentrate, yeast nutrient and activated yeast. Fit an airlock and ferment until finished and clear. Top up with water when the initial phase has calmed down.

LAVENDER WINE

This is quite an unusual-tasting wine and may not be to everyone's liking, but it is lovely served slightly chilled as an appetizer on a hot summer's day. The lavender taste develops over time and becomes an almost zesty, fresh flavor.

Ingredients

    4 fl oz (125 ml) dried lavender flowers
        (off stem)
    Half a lemon
    1 can of white grape concentrate
    2 lb (1 kg) sugar
    Wine yeast
    Yeast nutrient
    Water to make 5 quarts (5 liters) of wine

Method

1. Pour 1 quart (1 liter) of boiling water onto the dried lavender flowers and the chopped up lemon. Stand, covered, for 3 days, removing the lemon a few hours after you start.

2. Strain the lavender mixture into a demijohn. Dissolve the sugar in hot water

LOGANBERRY WINE

Loganberries (*Rubus loganobaccus*) are thought to be a wild cross between a blackberry and a raspberry. They develop large, light red berries that do not darken when ripe and possess a unique tart flavor. They make a truly exceptional wine that must age considerably if dry or a lot less if sweet.

Ingredients

    3 lb (1.3 kg) loganberries
    3 lb (1.3 kg) sugar
    Pectic enzyme
    1 campden tablet
    5 quarts (5 liters) water
    Citric acid
    Yeast nutrient
    Wine yeast

Method

1. Place the loganberries and sugar in a fermentation bucket and add the boiling water, stirring vigorously to dissolve the sugar.

2. When cool add the pectic enzyme, citric acid, yeast nutrient and wine yeast, and cover. Leave for 7 days in a warm place, stirring daily.

3. Strain and put into a demijohn with an airlock and seal the jar.

4. Store in a warm place and allow the fermentation to work.

5. When fermentation has ceased, rack the wine into a clean jar and leave in a cool place.

6. When the wine is clear and stable, siphon off into clean bottles.

NETTLE WINE

This is a great old English sweet wine that is very easy to make. Unless you really have tough skin on your hands, a pair of gloves is recommended for picking the nettles. Try to pick only the tops of the nettles for this recipe, as these tend to be a little sweeter.

Ingredients

   0.3 oz (10 g) ginger root (bruised)
   2 lemons
   2 quarts (2 liters) nettles
   3.75 lb (1.7 kg) sugar
   5 quarts (5 liters) water

Method

1. Wash the nettles thoroughly and drain off before use.

2. Bruise the ginger then add it to a pan along with the nettles, lemon peel and water and simmer for 50 minutes.

3. Strain and transfer to a bucket. Add the sugar and stir until it has dissolved.

4. Add more water to bring it back up to 5 quarts (5 liters), and wait until the temperature drops to 70°F (21°C) before adding the yeast.

5. Cover the bucket and put in a warm place for 4 days, before thoroughly stirring.

6. Now add to a fermentation vessel, fit an airlock and leave to stand for 2 months until it becomes clear.

OAK LEAF WINE

This is a highly successful wine made with young oak leaves, which are best picked during the last week of May or first week of June while they are still fresh. This very light wine is best drunk while it is still young.

Ingredients

   5 quarts (5 liters) oak leaves
   5 quarts (5 liters) water
   2 lb (1 kg) sugar
   Juice and rind of 3 oranges
   Yeast
   Pectic enzyme

Method

1. Boil the water and pour on top of the oak leaves, leaving overnight.

2. Strain out the leaves and boil the liquid for 20 minutes.

3. Add the sugar and orange juice and the grated rind.

4. When the liquid has cooled to 99°F (37°C), add the yeast and leave to ferment in an open bucket for 5 days.

5. Transfer to a fermentation jar. Fit an airlock and leave to ferment until it stops working and the sediment settles.

6. Siphon off into a clean jar and add pectic enzyme to remove the haze. Leave for 24 hours and then filter the wine off into sterilized bottles. Cork down with corks that have been boiled for 10 minutes.

PARSNIP WINE

Although parsnips might seem like an unlikely ingredient for making wine, they make a very palatable sweet wine with plenty of body. It keeps very well and is best made in February or March with parnips that have stayed in the ground all winter.

Ingredients

3.75 lb (1.7 kg) parsnips
3 lb (1.3 kg) white sugar
5 quarts (5 liters) cold water
1 lemon
Prepared juice of 0.5 lb (225 g) raisins
1 campden tablet
Pectic enzyme
Wine yeast and nutrient

Method

1. Prepare your raisins in advance of making the wine. Give them a brief wash in near boiling water to remove the waxy coat that the producers apply. Allow the raisins to cool enough to handle and then cut them up. Simmer the raisins in just enough water to cover them. After simmering for about 5 minutes, extract the juice from the raisins by means of a muslin cloth. Reserve for later use.

2. Scrub the parsnips well, but do not peel them. Slice them thinly and put them in a large saucepan or preserving pan. Pour in the water and cook the parsnips until they are tender, but not mushy. When they have cooled sufficiently, strain the liquid off and return this to the pan.

3. Add the sugar, the raisin juice and the lemon juice and rind, having removed all the pith. Simmer for 45 minutes, stirring occasionally.

4. Strain again into a plastic bucket, leave until lukewarm and add the pectic enzyme and crushed campden tablet. Leave for 24 hours, placing the bucket in a warm room.

5. Stir in the yeast and yeast nutrient, cover the bucket and leave in a warm room for a further 4 days, stirring well each day.

6. Strain into a fermentation jar. Fit with an airlock and ferment until the liquid becomes clear. Bottle and leave for 6 months or longer.

If fermentation seems slow you can feed the mixture with 2 tablespoons or so of sugar.

PEA POD WINE

Common garden pea pods contain varying amounts of sugar and have long been a base ingredient for wine. It really doesn't matter what type of pea you use for this recipe, but green fresh pods make the best wine. For a medium, German-type wine this recipe is an excellent choice.

Ingredients
2 lb (1 kg) pea pods
1 lb (450 g) sultanas
2 oranges
1/4 tsp citric acid
2 lb (1 kg) sugar
9.5 fl oz (280 ml) freshly made strong tea
Pectic enzyme
Wine yeast and nutrient
5 quarts (5 liters) water

Method
1. Thoroughly wash the pea pods and cut them up into small pieces. Put them in enough water to cover them well, bring slowly to the boil and simmer gently for 20 minutes with the lid on.
2. Put the sugar in a fermenting bucket with the chopped sultanas. Strain the boiling pea pods over the sugar and sultanas through three or four thicknesses of muslin. Allow to drain, squeezing out the maximum amount of liquid you can before discarding the pods.
3. Stir the mixture to dissolve the sugar, and make up to about 5 quarts (5 liters) with boiling water.
4. Add the citric acid and tea, cover closely and allow the mixture to cool to about 64°F, 18°C (lukewarm).
5. Halve the oranges, squeeze out the juice, strain and stir into the mixture. Then add the yeast, yeast nutrient and a few drops of pectic enzyme. Cover the vessel with polythene sheet or tight fitting lid, and tie this down tightly using thin, but strong, string. Put the vessel in a warm place to ferment for 10 days, stirring daily.
6. Now strain out all the solids through several thicknesses of muslin. Clean the fermenting vessel and return the strained liquid into this. Cover as before and leave in a warm place to ferment for a further 3 to 4 days.
7. Pour carefully into a 5-quart (5-liter) jar, leaving as much deposit in the bucket as you can. Fill the jar, to where the neck

begins, with boiled water that has been allowed to cool. Fit a fermentation lock and leave until all the fermentation has ceased before siphoning off into bottles.

————————

PEAR WINE

Pears make a wonderful wine, but depending on the type of pear used the final flavor will vary greatly. You may need to experiment with a few varieties before you get the final product to your liking.

Ingredients

    5 quarts (5 liters) boiling
        water
    3.75 lb (1.7 kg) pears
    2 tsp pectic enzyme
    2 lb (900 g) sugar
    2 lemons, juice only
    1 packet yeast
    3 tsp yeast nutrient
    1 campden tablet

Method

1. Pour the boiling water over the pears in a clean plastic bucket. Press down well on the pears to extract all their juice. Leave for 4 to 5 hours.
2. Add the pectic enzyme, cover and leave for 4 days to infuse.
3. Strain the pears through muslin and pour the liquid through a large funnel into a demijohn.
4. Add the sugar and lemon juice.
5. Add the yeast and yeast nutrient and fit an airlock. Leave in a warm room for about 7 to 10 days.
6. When the wine begins to clear and the bubbles have slowed down, siphon off the wine, leaving the debris in the bottom, into a clean demijohn.
7. After another 3 to 4 days, when all the fermentation has stopped, siphon off into a clean demijohn and add a campden tablet.
8. Stopper the jar and leave in a cool place for a further 10 days, by which time the wine should be clear.
9. Siphon the wine into clean bottles and store in a cool place. The wine should be ready for drinking after about 3 months.

————————

PLUM WINE

In plum wine, the quality of the final product reflects the quality of the fruit used. Use sour or overripe fruit, and the wine will be sour or bitter. Use firm, ripe fruit for the best quality wine. Any variety of plums can be used, but do not mix varieties. Black, or near black, seem to make the best wines.

Ingredients

    5 lb (2.25 kg) plums
    3 lb (1.3 kg) sugar
    5 quarts (5 liters) water

1 tsp citric acid
Wine yeast

Method

1. Wash and cut up the fruit and place in a fermentation bucket. Pour over the boiling water, cover bucket and leave for 4 days.
2. Stir twice daily and then strain on to the sugar, stirring vigorously until the sugar has dissolved. Add the yeast and cover.
3. Stir regularly for 5 days and then pour into a fermentation bottle. Fit an airlock and leave to finish fermenting.
4. When fermentation has ceased, siphon the wine into a clean jar and place in a cool room for a few months.
5. Siphon off again if necessary and leave until the wine is stable, before bottling.

This wine can take up to 12 months to mature.

POTATO WINE

Strange as it may seem, a very nice wine can be made with potatoes. When potatoes are being dug, put aside the little ones that are too small for cooking as they work very well for this purpose. King Edward potatoes work exceedingly well for this recipe.

Ingredients

3.5 lb (1.5 kg) potatoes
3.5 lb (1.5 kg) sugar
8 fl oz (250) ml grape concentrate

1 mug of cold tea with no added milk or sugar
5 quarts (5 liters) water
1 tsp citric acid
1 tsp yeast nutrient
Wine yeast
1 campden tablet and potassium sorbate

Method

1. Wash and scrub the potatoes, cutting out any eyes or green bits. Leave the skin on as this helps to improve the flavor. Grate them or chop them up finely, cover with water immediately, otherwise they will go brown.
2. Boil the potatoes for about 15 minutes, skimming off any skum from the surface.
3. Strain through a sieve or muslin into a clean bucket. Add the sugar and stir until it has dissolved.
4. Top up to about 4 quarts (4 liters) of liquid with water and leave overnight.
5. Add the rest of the ingredients and stir well. Pour into a demijohn, add an airlock and leave until vigorous frothing subsides. Top up to the shoulder of the demijohn with cold water.
6. When bubbles stop coming through the airlock, or slow down to about one every 2 minutes, test the wine. You can either use a hydrometer or just taste it. If you like the taste, then you can proceed to the next step.
7. When the wine has stopped fermenting, add 1 campden tablet and potassium sorbate and leave to clear.

8. When the wine is clear, siphon into a clear demijohn. If it is too dry at this stage you can sweeten it with a little sugar, but make sure that it doesn't start to ferment again. Leave it for a couple of weeks and then add a campden tablet before bottling.

RASPBERRY WINE

This is a really special wine with a sharp, distinct flavor that doesn't necessarily improve with keeping.

Ingredients
    26 oz (750 g) raspberries
    2 lb (1 kg) sugar
    2 oranges
    Wine yeast
    2 campden tablets
    5 quarts (5 liters) water

Method
1. Pick over the raspberries, removing any unripe fruit, and place in a plastic bucket.
2. Pour over 3 quarts (3 liters) of boiling water, then mash the fruit up well with a wooden spoon. Add 1 crushed campden tablet. Leave for 2 days then strain off the liquid through a muslin, pressing well to get the fruit juice through.
3. Add the juice of the oranges.
4. Boil up the rest of the water with the sugar and add it to the liquid.
5. Start the yeast and add it to the mixture when it has cooled to lukewarm.

6. Leave to ferment in the bucket for 3 days, then move to a fermenting jar with an airlock. Leave it to ferment untill all the working has stopped.
7. Filter and add a crushed campden tablet. Taste it. If it is too dry, you can sweeten it with a very small amount of sugar syrup.
8. Bottle in sterilized bottles and store in a cool place.

RHUBARB WINE

This is a wine that would have been very familiar to country folk in 19th-century England. It is best made in the middle of May when rhubarb is at its best.

Ingredients
    3 lb (1.25 kg) rhubarb
    3 lb (1.25 kg) sugar
    1 packet wine yeast
    5 quarts (5 liters) water
    1 cup cold black tea
    2 campden tablets

Method
1. Wipe the rhubarb with a wet cloth, but do not peel. Chop into small pieces and cover with sugar in a large bowl.
2. Leave overnight until the sugar has completely dissolved.
3. Strain off the syrup and cover the rhubarb with water to rinse off any remaining sugar. Add this liquid to the syrup and make it up to 5 quarts (5 liters)

with water and a cup of cold black tea to add astringency.

4. Add the wine yeast and transfer the liquid to a demijohn fitted with an airlock. Leave to ferment.

5. Using a hydrometer, stop fermentation using 2 campden tablets when the reading reaches about 1.010.

6. Leave the wine to clear naturally.

7. Siphon the wine into sterilized bottles and leave for a minimum of 3 months. If kept in a cool place, this wine may be stored for up to 2 years.

This wine will improve greatly by keeping, and should be a very brilliant color.

ROSEHIP WINE

Rosehips develop on rose bushes slowly during the summer, turn orange in late August and September, and are ready to pick when they turn red.

The bottled wine must mature for at least 2 years to reach its potential, as young rosehip wine will be almost undrinkable.

Ingredients

2 lb (1 kg) rosehips
2 lb (1 kg) sugar
Juice of 1 lemon and 1 orange
5 quarts (5 liters) water
Wine yeast

Method

1. Mince the freshly gathered rosehips—make sure you pick them after the first frost. Place the minced rosehips into a bucket and pour on boiling water. Stir with a long-handled spoon. Do not use your hand because of the itchy hairs inside the hips. Allow this to stand for 3 days, stirring daily.

2. Strain through a wine bag or several layers of muslin. Make up the sugar syrup, add to the wine juice and place it in a fermentation jar.

3. Make up the yeast and allow it to work. Then add to the wine.

4. Make up the amount of liquid to within 1 in (3 cm) of the top of the jar with boiled, cooled water. Fit an airlock and leave to work until clear.

5. Siphon into a clean container and keep for another 3 months, before bottling.

ROWAN WINE

The Rowan or Mountain Ash (*Sorbus aucuparia*) is a small, deciduous tree. The berries have been used in drinks for centuries and should be picked in October when they have reached their full color, but have not yet become mushy.

Ingredients

2 lb (1 kg) rowan berries
2 oranges
2 quarts (2 liters) boiling water
3 lb (1.3 kg) sugar
Wine yeast

Method

1. Pick the berries when ripe, making sure you remove all the stalks. Wash carefully and put into a white plastic bucket. Pour on 2 quarts (2 liters) of boiling water. Don't worry about the smell at this stage of the proceedings.
2. Leave the must for 3 days, stirring daily. Strain through a muslin cloth or bag into a demijohn.
3. Making up the sugar syrup with 3 lb (1.3 kg) sugar and 29 fl oz (850 ml) water. Pour into the jar, grate the orange rind and squeeze juice into the jar. Start yeast fermenting, and add to the wine.
4. Put a cotton wool bung into the neck of the jar and leave for 3 days.
5. Put on an airlock and leave to ferment for about 4 months. This wine clears very quickly.
6. Siphon into a clean jar and leave for at least 6 months.

It is a long time before this wine becomes drinkable, so leave it for as long as you can.

————•••◦•••————

SLOE WINE

Sloes are the blue-black, tart fruit of the blackthorn tree (*Prunus spinosa*). Wild sloes make an excellent wine but, like cherry wine, it must be aged for some time to allow it to come into its own. When fermentation ends, the wine will not be very palatable, but don't be tempted to sweeten it at this stage. Simply put the wine in a cool, dark place and forget about it for at least another year.

Ingredients

3 lb (1.25 kg) sloes
2 lb (1 kg) sugar
2 oranges
5 quarts (5 liters) water
Wine yeast
1 campden tablet

Method

1. Boil the sloes in half of the water for about 20 minutes, crushing them with a wooden spoon to break the skins. Strain off the solids and put the liquid into a plastic bucket.
2. Start the yeast.
3. Boil the sugar in the other half of the water until it has dissolved and squeeze in the juice of the two oranges. Add the crushed campden tablet.
4. When the liquid has cooled down, add the yeast and leave to ferment in the bucket for 4 days.
5. Transfer to a fermentation jar and leave to ferment until it clears—approximately 3 months—before bottling.

The final result will depend entirely on the quality of the sloes. Some years the result will be extremely dry and will need sweetening with a little sugar syrup.

STRAWBERRY WINE

With a perfect blend of the freshest and sweetest strawberries, this is one of the most delicate and exquisite wines you can make at home. You will need to plan this one in advance if you are thinking of serving it for a special occasion, as strawberry wines need to age for at least 1 year.

Ingredients

6.5 lb (3 kg) whole fresh strawberries, washed and hulled

9.5 quarts (9 liters) boiling water

Juice of 1 lemon

5 lb (2.25 kg) sugar

Method

1. In a large earthenware crock, mash the strawberries. Cover with boiling water and add the lemon juice. Stir quickly for about 2 minutes. Cover with a clean linen cloth and leave in a cool, dark place, stirring daily for 1 week.

2. Strain the mixture through a double layer of muslin into a large, clean bowl, discarding the strawberry pulp.

3. Combine the strawberry liquid with the sugar, stirring until the sugar has dissolved. Pour into a clean crock and leave it to stand for another week, stirring daily.

4. Pour the strawberry liquid into demijohns and put an airlock in place. Leave it to rest in a cool, dark place for 3 months.

5. When the wine is clear and no longer fermenting, pour into individual bottles and cork. Leave it for at least 1 year before attempting to drink this delicious wine.

TOMATO WINE (RED)

You will probably find you have a glut of tomatoes toward the end of the summer, and this refreshing wine is a great way of using them up.

Ingredients

5 lb (2.25 kg) ripe tomatoes

2 lb (1 kg) sugar

Juice of 2 lemons

½ tsp pectic enzyme

Wine yeast and nutrient

5 quarts (5 liters) water

1 campden tablet

Method

1. Wash and chop the tomatoes. Add to a fermenting bucket, together with all the other ingredients with the exception of the

yeast. Stir thoroughly and leave to settle overnight.

2. Add activated wine yeast and stir the tomato must twice a day for 5 days.

3. Strain the tomato mixture thoroughly, extracting all of the juice and liquor. Transfer into a demijohn, with an airlock.

4. Siphon for the first time at 4 weeks, and then two or three times more until the liquid is clear and 1 year old.

5. Bottle the tomato wine and leave to stand for a few months before drinking.

WASSAIL WINE

It seems fitting to end this section with a fruity, spicy wine for Christmas.

Ingredients

3 lb (1.3 kg) mixed dried fruit

Muslin bag of mixed spices—cinnamon sticks, whole allspice lightly crushed, mace, shavings of nutmeg and 2 cloves

2 large oranges chopped

Grated zest of two tangerines

3 quarts (3 liters) boiling water

Pectic enzyme

Citric acid

Wine yeast and nutrient

Can of red grape concentrate

2 lb (1 kg) sugar

Method

1. Bring the water to a boil and add the spice bag. Simmer for a few minutes. Add oranges, tangerine zest and mixed fruit and simmer for a further 10 minutes.

2. Allow to cool and transfer to a fermenting bucket. Add pectic enzyme and citric acid and leave overnight.

3. Remove orange pieces and discard, squeezing them first to extract juice. Then squeeze the mixed fruit.

4. Dissolve the sugar in hot water and add to the bucket when cooled.

5. Activate the yeast and add to the bucket with yeast nutrient and grape concentrate.

6. Stir well, cover, and leave for 5 days, stirring and squeezing the fruit daily.

7. Strain off through muslin or a sieve into a sterilized demijohn, and fit an airlock.

8. When the fermentation process is complete, siphon off into bottles and leave until Christmas.

As this can be quite messy when you get to the straining stage, you might like to have the mixed fruit in a jelly-straining bag at the fermenting stage, which will make life a lot easier.

Mead, Cider
and Perry

MEAD

Mead is very possibly the oldest alcoholic drink in the world. The mere mention of the word conjures up visions of drinking vessels swaying high in the air, with merry Vikings singing their rowdy songs into the early hours of the morning. Mead is the nectar of nectars, and one of the most natural drinks ever made by man.

Mead is a pleasant alcoholic drink made from diluted honey and water, which is then fermented by yeast. Because nature created mead naturally without the intervention of man, it makes sense that we would develop the ability to recreate this drink. Indeed, mankind's first experiences with intoxication could easily have sprung from the spontaneous fermentation of honey in some old tree trunk containing a bee hive. The hive could have become sodden with rainwater, and fermentation initiated by the wild yeasts that are around us in the air every day. The pleasant effects of this wild elixir would probably have seemed magical to primitive man.

Early cave paintings have shown the collection of honey from hives, although it is uncertain what it was used for. Gradually, through the centuries, the drinking of intoxicating beverages became part of man's culture, with rituals and traditions surrounding the making and drinking of these substances.

Fermentation served another purpose as well. Water was not safe to drink and needed to be purified—so fermentation was used . The process by which wine, beer and mead is made destroys many pathogens that can make water unsafe.

Some of the original meads were heavily spiced to cover up the flavors of fermentation contamination. It wasn't until the mid-1800s that yeast was discovered as a natural fermenter, so up until this time the process was a bit hit or miss.

It was the Scandinavians that showed us the way when it came to making mead. They believed it to be the spirit of love and our own word honeymoon comes from the wedding celebrations of the Norse. They danced and drank mead until there wasn't a drop left—woe betide the host who didn't have enough supplies to last the full cycle of the moon.

The Norse also believed that mead was responsible for human fertility and the birth of sons. It was believed that if mead was drunk for 1 whole month after a wedding, then the first child born would be a male. This was very important to their society in helping to build up the powerful Norse clans. If a couple was successful in raising a son, then thanks would be offered by the clan to the maker of the mead as well as to the groom, who could now boast of his virility.

Although this might seem a little far-fetched, in actual fact the acidity and sweetness of the drink can influence the mother-to-be's body acidity, which in turn can influence the sex of the unborn baby.

Other traditions called for the use of communal cups, or mazers, which were large, open vessels about the size of a chalice. This would be passed from hand to hand, with each participant offering a toast or prayer as it was passed to the next person.

In ancient times, the making of mead was believed to be a magical craft, not fully understand by the peasants. It was an arcane type of magic that was regulated by custom, law and superstition, and only certain individuals were trained in the art of turning the juice of grape, the toil of the bee and the grain from the field into a mind-altering substance.

The most famous mead-makers in the world reside on the island of Lindisfarne in the British Isles, where mead has been manufactured continuously since the end of the Roman occupation.

Now it is time for you to experiment and form your own kind of magic. Try some of these recipes for mead and then you can experience the magic of this historic beverage.

VARIANTS OF MEAD

Braggot
Also called bracket or brackett, this marks the invention of true ale. Originally brewed with honey and hops, later with honey and malt—with or without the addition of hops.

Black mead
A name sometimes given to the blend of honey and blackcurrants.

Cyser
A fermented apple juice and honey, perhaps a forerunner of cider.

Great mead
Any mead that is intended to be aged several years like vintage wine.

Hydromel
This is a name used for very light, or low-alcohol mead.

Melomel
This is made from honey and any fruit.

Metheglin
This is a spiced variety that was supposed to have medicinal powers.

Morat

This is a blend of honey and mulberries.

Oxymel

Another old mead recipe, blending honey with wine vinegar.

Pyment

Pyment blends honey and red or white grapes. Pyment made with white grape juice is sometimes called white mead.

Rhodomel

Rhodomel is made from honey, rosehips, petals, or rose attar and water.

Sack mead

This refers to mead that is made with more copious amounts of honey than usual.

Short mead

Also called quick mead. A type of mead recipe that is meant to age quickly, for immediate consumption.

Show mead

A term that has come to mean plain mead; that which has honey and water as a base, with no fruits, spices or extra flavorings.

BASIC MEAD BREWING

This is a classic British method for brewing mead and this recipe takes you through every step you need to brew a mead from scratch. As with making ale, sterility is an essential prerequisite of making mead. So make sure you sanitize everything that comes into contact with any of the ingredients.

Ingredients

    5 quarts (5 liters) unchlorinated water
    3.5 lb (1.5 kg) honey
    1 tsp acid blend
    1 tsp yeast nutrient
    1 packet champagne yeast

The acid blend gives the finished mead a subtle fruitiness and balanced taste. The yeast nutrient helps the yeast develop more quickly, as honey does not contain the amino acids that yeast needs to thrive.

Method

1. Prepare your yeast. If you are using dried yeast, boil some water and pour 7 fl oz (200 ml) into a shallow dish, stirring in 4 tablespoons of honey. Cover with tin foil and allow to cool naturally to just below 99°F (37°C). Sprinkle the yeast over the surface of the water and leave to rehydrate for 10 minutes. At the end of this time, gently stir the yeast and set aside in a warm place for at least 2 hours.

2. Measure the volume of water needed by filling a demijohn two-thirds full of water (about 3 quarts, 3 liters) and then pour into a stainless steel brewing pot. Bring this to a rolling boil and take off the heat.

3. Begin stirring in the honey. Next, add the

acid blend and the yeast nutrient. Be careful when adding the honey to make sure that it dissolves quickly and does not burn on the base of the pot. Also be very careful that the mixture does not boil over and scald you.

4. Cover the pot with some clean tin foil and allow to cool naturally to about 99°F (37°C). Place a sterile funnel In your demijohn and pour in the honey mixture. Stir your yeast starter mixture and pour this into the demijohn. Swirl this to mix the ingredients and then close with a bung and a fermentation airlock. Set the demijohn in a warm place and wait.

5. Within the next 24 hours, the airlock will start bubbling rapidly and foam should be forming on top of the liquid. These are the essential signs you need to see to know that your batch of mead Is progressing.

6. Place in a cool, dark area and monitor every day to check on its progress. Over the next few weeks the bubbling should start to slow down and a layer of sediment will build up on the bottom of the demijohn. When this sediment is somewhere about 1 in (2.5 cm) deep, it is time to rack your mead. Racking is simply the process of siphoning the liquid off the sediment into a clean, sterilized demijohn. **This stage is important, as leaving your developing mead on the sediment too long can taint its flavor.**

7. Now you are ready for the second stage of fermentation. During racking make sure you disturb the liquid as little as possible, then carefully top up the new demijohn with fresh water so that it is full up to the neck. Sterilize a bung, and plug the neck of the demijohn with this and a fermentation lock. Try to expose your mead to as little oxygen as possible.

8. Continue to check your demijohn each day. If the layer of sediment builds up to the original level, you will need to rack the liquid again. If the level of liquid falls below the neck of the demijohn, top it up with water. If a week or two goes by and you don't see any more bubbles in the airlock, then the fermentation is over. This could take as long as 6 months.

9. Now is the time to bottle your mead and leave it to age.

BRAGGOT (ALE MEAD)

This is unusual as it is a high-strength mead that uses some of the ingredients used in making ales.

Ingredients

5 quarts (5 liters) unchlorinated water
4 lb (2 kg) wildflower honey
3.5 lb (1.5 kg) light malt extract
2 lemons, sliced
1 oz (30 g) Cascade finishing hops (see
    Beer section)
1 oz (30 g) Fuggles finishing hops
Yeast

Method

1. Follow the instructions given in the basic mead recipe. At the boiling stage, add the finishing hops. Take the pot off the heat after 5 minutes and remove the hops.

2. Add the sliced lemon and keep in the mixture for 30 minutes. Remove the lemon, allow the must to cool and continue as normal.

This mead should be left to mature for at least 1 year once bottled.

BLACKBERRY MEAD

This is a traditional British recipe for a classic fruit-flavored mead (metheglin), that uses blackberries for flavoring.

Ingredients

5 quarts (5 liters) unchlorinated water
12 lb (5.5 kg) honey
2 lb (1 kg) fresh blackberries
Pared zest of 2 oranges
4 tsp yeast nutrient
6 tsp pectic enzyme
Yeast

Method

1. Prepare the blackberries by boiling with 6.5 lb (3 kg) honey and 2 quarts (2 liters) of water until soft and mushy.

2. In a separate pan, combine 3 quarts (3 liters) unchlorinated water and 6 lb (2.75 kg) honey. When the honey has dissolved mix in the blackberry mix. Stir in the orange zest and yeast nutrient, then pour into your fermentation bucket. Cover and allow to cool to room temperature. Stir in the pectic enzyme and set aside for 12 hours.

3. Add the yeast and cover. Set aside in a warm place to ferment for about 8 days, stirring every day until vigorous fermentation subsides.

4. Strain the liquid into a demijohn, then make up to 5 quarts (5 liters) with more water. Fit a bung and a fermentation lock and leave to ferment in a warm, dark place for 60 to 90 days, or until all fermentation has ceased.

5. Rack the wine into a second fermentation jar, add a bung and a fermentation lock and set aside for about 45 days.

6. Rack once more into a clean demijohn and set aside in a cool, dark place for a further 45 days, or until it clarifies.

7. Rack the mead into bottles and cork securely. Lay the bottles down in a cool place and leave to mature for at least 6 months. If you can be patient, this mead will age and develop over 2 years.

CHRISTMAS MELOMEL MEAD

This is a classic British mead that is flavored with cranberries and citrus peel and is designed to be drunk at Christmas.

Ingredients

3 quarts (3 liters) unchlorinated water
6.5 lb (3 kg) honey
25 oz (700 g) fresh cranberries
Pared peel of 2 oranges
6 tsp yeast nutrient
6 tsp pectic enzyme
Yeast

Method

1. First prepare the cranberries by boiling in 6.5 lb (3 kg) honey and 2 quarts (2 liters) of water until they pop and go translucent.

2. Follow the recipe for basic mead and then add the cranberry mixture to the boiling honey and water mixture. When you have completed the boil, add the pared orange peel, pectin and yeast nutrient and allow to infuse until the must cools. At this point take out the orange peel.

3. At this point return to the instructions for the basic mead recipe. Once bottled, this should be left to mature for at least 1 year before drinking.

MIDSUMMER MEAD

This is another classic British mead that incorporates wild flowers and herbs as flavorings for the honey base.

Ingredients

5 quarts (5 liters) unchlorinated water
17 fl oz (500 ml) honey
17 fl oz (500 ml) meadowsweet leaves
  (packed)
3.25 oz (90 g) brown sugar
17 fl oz (500 ml) woodruff sprigs
  (packed)
18 oz (500 g) barley malt
17 fl oz (500 ml) heather flowers, packed
3 cloves
Yeast

Method

1. Follow the instructions in the basic mead recipe. Pour the water into a large pot, bring to the boil, then add the meadowsweet, woodruff, heather and cloves. Boil for 1 hour, then add the honey, brown sugar and barley malt. Stir until everything has dissolved, then cover with a lid and leave to cool overnight.

2. In the morning strain through muslin, then add the yeast and prepare the must as usual. The first racking should be done after about a month and the second after fermentation stops completely. Mature for 1 year.

OAK LEAF MELOMEL MEAD

Oak leaf mead is a classic medieval Welsh mead. It uses oak leaves as a bittering agent and raisins to provide the fruit for the melomel.

Ingredients

    5 quarts (5 liters) of unchlorinated water
    9 lb (4 kg) honey
    18 oz (500 g) chopped raisins
    Sufficient clean brown withered oak
        leaves gathered from the tree on a dry
        day to fill a 5-quart (5-liter) bucket
    6 tsp yeast nutrient
    1 large piece of bruised ginger
    Yeast (Epernay II is good)

Method

1. Pour 5 quarts (5 liters) of boiling water over the oak leaves in a fermenting bucket. Cover and leave to infuse for 4 to 5 days. At the end of this time strain the liquid through muslin, into a large stock pot.

2. Add the raisins and ginger to this oak-leaf infusion, bring to the boil and add the honey a little at a time until it dissolves. Then add the yeast nutrient (this is not strictly necessary but will help kick-start the fermentation).

3. Take the must off the heat, remove the ginger, and allow to cool. At this point you can return to following the basic mead instructions to finish making your mead.

Once bottled, this mead needs to be left to mature in the bottle for at least a year.

MODERN MEAD

Depending on how sweet or dry you like your mead use about 3.5 lb (1.5 kg) of honey for a dry wine or about 3.75 lb (1.7 kg) for a sweet one.

Ingredients

    3.5-3.75 lb (1.5-1.7 kg) set honey
    20 fl oz (591 ml) cold tea
    Campden tablets
    1 tsp citric acid
    Wine yeast compound or special mead
        yeast and yeast nutrient

Method

1. Dissolve the honey over a low heat. Add the tea and 1 campden tablet dissolved in 5 fl oz (140 ml) of boiling water. Place in a 5-quart (5-liter) fermentation vessel. Top up to almost three-quarters full with boiled water and shake to mix thoroughly. Add the citric acid.

2. Prepare the yeast starter. When must (starter) has been fermenting for about 3 to 5 hours it should be added to the fermentation vessel. Ensure it is mixed well and top up with more cooled water. Fit an airlock and put in a warm place to ferment.

WATCH IT CAREFULLY

3. If heavy sediment builds up, siphon the mead into a seperate vessel, taking just a little of the sediment. When fermentation is complete (4 to 6 weeks) siphon the mead into a clean, sterilized vessel i.e. no sediment

4. See campden tablet instructions. Dissolve 1 or 2 tablets in a little hot water and add to the mead. This will ensure fermentation cecases and that the mead clears.

5. Leave sealed under an airlock until the mead is cleared and sediment has formed. Bottle in sterilized bottles, cork and label.

Store for at least 6 to 12 months—the longer the better.

IRISH NETTLE MEAD

This mead is a bright green color from the nettle juice. It is based on an old Irish recipe and is a great drink to bring out on St Patrick's Day.

Ingredients

2 quarts (2 liters) young stinging nettle heads
4 quarts (4 liters) water
3 oranges, cut into segments (including peel)
3 lemons, cut into segments (including peel)
4 lb (2 kg) honey
8.5 oz (240 g) hops
12.5 oz (360 g) ginger, bruised
2 nutmegs, quartered
6 Tbsp allspice berries
0.5 oz (15 g) yeast
1 piece of toast

Method

1. Combine the nettle heads, water, oranges and lemons in a large pot. Bring the mixture to a boil and then simmer for 40 minutes. Take off the heat and strain through a muslin bag.

2. Return the liquid to the pan, bring back to a boil then add the honey and bring back to the boil. Continue boiling for 1 hour, skimming the surface as any scum rises.

3. Add the spices and hops and boil for a further 10 minutes.

4. Strain the liquid through a muslin bag into a fermenting bucket. Cover and allow to cool until it is lukewarm (99°F, 37°C).

5. Spread a piece of toast with 0.5 oz (15 g) yeast and float this on the surface of the liquid. Leave to ferment for 3 days, then skim the surface and transfer to a fermenting bottle with an airlock.

6. When fermentation has stopped (about 2 weeks) and no more bubbles can be seen, rack into bottles. Stopper the bottles securely then lay down in a cool place. The mead will be ready to drink in 3 to 6 months, but can be kept much longer.

PLUM MEAD

This makes a lovely light, rosé-type mead.

Ingredients

    2 lb (1 kg) plums (late variety)
    8 lb (3.5 kg) honey
    Cinnamon stick
    1 lemon
    2 quarts (2 liters) water
    1 crushed campden tablet
    Yeast and yeast nutrient

Method

1. Soak the plums in a solution of crushed campden tablet and cold water for 1 hour to kill off any wild yeast on the skins.

2. Boil the water and add the honey, reducing it to a gentle simmer. Skim any scum off the surface and continue to simmer for approximately 30 minutes.

3. Halve and remove the pits from the plums, discarding any bruised or damaged fruit.

4. Cool the honey/water mixture to room temperature, then add the plums, juice and quartered rind of the lemon and finally the cinnamon stick.

5. Activate the yeast and add to the plum mixture. Add the yeast nutrient.

6. Transfer to a fermenting bucket and stand in a warm place for a few days, stirring daily.

7. When the first vigorous fermentation has slowed down, strain the mixture through muslin into a demijohn. Squeeze the plum pulp to extract the liquid, but don't overdo it as you will make the liquid too cloudy. Fit a fermentation lock and leave in a warm place to ferment.

8. After a couple of weeks rack into a clean demijohn. Continue to rack and monitor the gravity level until the mead clears. Make sure the fermentation has completely finished, as mead is notorious for false stops.

CIDER

It is the end of the summer and apples are in abundance. Some people are deterred from making cider because they think it is a complicated process, but the only ingredient you need to get started is apples. A mixture of good eating apples and some cookers will make an acceptable drink, so why not have a go—it's not as hard as you might think.

Apples were first grown in Britain by Iron Age Celts and the Romans introduced some improved varieties. There is evidence of cider being made in the 1st century AD around the Mediterranean. By the 8th century it was well established in Brittany and Normandy and the first recorded production dates from 1205.

Although it is uncertain when the first cider was brewed in Britain, it is evident that the Norman Conquest of 1066 brought the most profound changes to apple-growing in Britain. The Normans had a strong tradition of both apple-growing and cider-making, introducing many different varieties of apple to Britain. The first recorded types were the Pearmain and the Costard. The Pearmain was particularly valued for cider making. By the 17th century, not only had cider become a hugely popular drink, but it was championed as the equal of even the best French wines.

In America, during the colonial period, cider was one of the most popular drinks and retained its popularity until the early 1900s, when prohibition resulted in a drastic decline in cider consumption. After prohibition was lifted, cider became a product of mass production. During the late 1900s, however, a noticeable revival began, with the ressurection of many of the traditional cidermaking methods.

THE PRINCIPLES OF FERMENTATION

In order to obtain cider from apples the fruit needs to go through two different types of fermentation. The first process is to add yeast artificially or allow the apples to ferment with the yeast naturally present on their skin. This allows the sugars to convert into ethanol, producing the alcoholic content of the cider. The second fermentation takes place in the juice of the apples where natural bacteria are already present. It converts the malic acid to lactic acid and carbon dioxide.

THE CIDER-MAKING PROCESS

Like any process using fruit, the first job is to pick or collect the fruit. The apples are not used immediately, but allowed to mature for a week before being tipped into a scratcher or scratter. This piece of equipment crushes the apples into a pulp, which at the early stages is referred to as pomace or pommy.

The next process is to extract the juice from the pulp, which is carried out using a cider press. There are several types of press used commercially, but it is not difficult to find complete cider press kits if you wish to buy one.

Alternatively, if you are good at do-it-yourself projects you can have a go at making one yourself.

TYPES OF APPLES

Cider apples, unlike eating apples, are high in acids and tannins. The major acid present is malic acid, but it is the tannin that gives the cider its color. The more tannin present, the deeper the color. Tannin is also responsible for the dryness of the cider and the characteristic taste that sits at the back of your tongue after drinking.

Cider apples fall into four separate categories depending on the levels of sugar, tannin and acid present.

Bittersweets—these are high in tannin but low in acid.
Sweets—these are low in both tannin and acid.
Bittersharps—these are high in both tannin and acid.
Sharps—these are low in tannin but high in acid.

The ideal cider apple contains a combination of all the above. So it is a good idea to seek advice from a professional, if possible, or read up on the best apples to use as there are more than 300 varieties.

MAKE YOUR OWN CIDER

If you don't want to go to the bother of extracting the apple juice yourself, you can always take it to a commercial press and get them to do it for you. This recipe uses 80 lb (36 kg) of mixed dessert apples and about 12 lb (5.5 kg) of crab apples. Approximately 24 lb (11 kg) of apples will make 5 quarts (5 liters) of apple juice.

1. The first task is to wash all the apples.

You might find this job easier outdoors, using a hose and something like an old trashcan. Discard any apples that are starting to rot and any pieces of branch or leaves that are attached to them.

2. Cut up the apples and pulp with a piece of hardwood (or pulp with a Pulpmaster). Make sure you discard any bruised apples.

3. Once pulped, press the pulp using a wine press or strain through a coarse straining bag. At this stage it is advisable to use a hydrometer to test the original gravity of the apples. The starting gravity ideal for cider is 1.050/1.055. If the SG is low, then add white granulated sugar to adjust it.

4. Pour the juice into a 5-quart (5-liter) glass demijohn, then add some wine yeast to start the fermentation. If you keep it at approximately 167°F (75°C), fermentation will take between 3 and 4 weeks. During this time it is a good idea to siphon off into a clean demijohn to clear any sediment.

5. For still cider, once it is clear it can be racked off into a clean demijohn. Add 1 crushed campden tablet to preserve the cider and leave to mature for at least 3 months.

6. For carbonated cider, with the hydrometer at 1.010, this can be bottled in any bottle that has previously held pressure—plastic PET bottles, beer bottles, champagne bottles, but not wine bottles, as these are not designed to withstand pressure. After a few weeks in a cool place, the cider should be clear, but should be allowed to mature for at least 3 months.

SCRUMPY

Scrumpy is the name often given to a traditional cider that is produced in the south and west of England. Its true heartland lies in a band through Devon, Somerset, Gloucestershire and Herefordshire. The name is derived from the obsolete dialect word *scrimp*, which literally means "a withered apple." From this word we get the verb *scrump*, which originally referred to the custom of collecting windfalls.

Scrumpy differs from regular cider in a number of ways. It is fermented naturally from whole apples rather than apple juice, contains no added sugar and is not pasteurized or carbonated. Some commercially sold scrumpy can be quite potent, reaching as high as 15 percent ABV.

MAKE YOUR OWN SCRUMPY

Here is a recipe for a strong scrumpy. You should let it mature for 1 year to become smoother and mellower.

Ingredients
8 lb (3.5 kg) apples, any type will do
11 quarts (10 liters) water
1 oz (28 g) root ginger
Juice of 4 lemons

Method

1. Cut up the unpeeled apples roughly with a non-metallic knife. **You must not use any metal in this recipe.** Cover with 10 quarts (9 liters) of boiling water preferably in a brewer's bucket.

2. Leave the mixture for 2 weeks, returning to crush the apples well now and again. Be careful that mold does not form at this stage.

3. Boil a pot of water. Strain the liquid and add the bruised root ginger and lemon juice. Give it a good stir to ensure that everything is thoroughly combined.

4. Add 1 quart (1 liter) of boiling water and leave the whole thing to stand again for just over 2 weeks, removing the scum off the top as it rises.

5. You will need two people for this next bit. Strain into resealable bottles and screw on the tops lightly for 2 days, just to the point where they would need another half turn to fully close them.

6. After about 5 weeks, tighten the stoppers and keep in a cool, dark and most importantly, dry place for 2 months.

TURBO CIDER

Turbo cider is exactly what its name suggests—one that is very quick and easy to make. It uses pure apple juice as opposed to whole apples, eliminating the messy business of preparing your own apples.

Ingredients

    5 quarts (5 liters) pure apple juice
    1 0.3 oz (6 g) packet of yeast (wine yeast
        is fine)
    Sugar/honey (optional)

Method

1. Sterilize everything you are going to use.

2. Pour 3 quarts (3 liters) of apple juice into a clean demijohn.

3. Place the yeast in the demijohn. Give it a good shake, add a bung and airlock and leave for about 36 hours to ferment.

4. Add the remainder of the apple juice.

5. Leave to ferment; ensure that the starting gravity is constant for at least 3 days.

If you like a stronger cider, you can add about 3 oz (80 g) of sugar and 2 to 3 teaspoons of honey. This should give you a

PERRY

Perry has been common for centuries in Britain, particularly the West Country and Wales, and in France, especially Normandy and Anjou. The basic processes for making cider and perry are very similar; however, the differences are important. Perry is made from pear juice that has undergone the same fermentation processes as cider apples.

The earliest reference to the use of pears for making an alcoholic drink was by Pliny who said that the Falernian variety, being very juicy, was used for making wine. In the 4th century, Palladius wrote of pears being used like apples to make a drink, and that Romans preferred wine made from pears to that of apples.

Like cider, the process starts with the picking of the fruit in this case, pears. These are left to mature for a period of 2 days to 1 week, depending on the variety used. This period is very important because if you do not leave the pears long enough very little of their flavor will be imparted to the perry. If you leave the fruit for too long, then it starts to rot from the middle outward and this can consequently go unnoticed. When the pears are ripened to perfection they are crushed, using exactly the same process as that used for apples in cider-making. However, unlike the cider-making process, with perry it is essential that the milled pomace is left to stand for a period before it is pressed. This is done to allow the pomace to lose its tannins so that it will produce a clear finished drink. The usual period for standing is overnight up to 24 hours. Then the pulp can be crushed to extract the juice, just as in a cider press.

The pressed juice is then fermented in exactly the same way as the apple juice used in cider making. The perry is matured in large storage tanks.

The true and traditional perry is served completely flat and sometimes appears cloudy. Pears tend to have a higher sugar content than cider apples. The acid composition also differs substantially from that of cider apples. Many pears contain quite large amounts of citric acid and malic acid, but again this depends on the variety of pear used.

PEAR TYPES
The quality of your perry will depend entirely on the type of pear used. They

come in the following categories: Sweet, Medium, Sharp, Bittersweet and Bittersharp.

Sweet pears have a low acidity, about 0.2 percent weight per volume (w/v) and fairly low tannin content at below 0.15 percent (w/v).

Medium Sharp pears have an acidity of between 0.2 and 0.6 percent (w/v) and a tannin content of below 0.15 percent (w/v).

Bittersweet pears have an acidity below 0.45 percent (w/v) and a tannin content of above 0.2 percent (w/v), but it is fair to say very few pears fall into this category.

Bittersharp (or astringent) pears have an acidity above 0.45 percent (w/v) and a tannin content above 0.2 percent (w/v). These pears have a penetrating flavor that is very striking, as the tannin is astringent rather than bitter. This type of pear is not suitable for eating but makes a wonderful perry.

Usually perries are made from a blend of pears, but if you choose to make one from a single variety then the bittersharp varieties are by far the best. These include: Barland, Green Longdon, Holmer, Moorcroft, Oldfield, Pint, Rock and Teddington Green.

MAKING YOUR OWN PERRY

Having matured your chosen pears for the correct amount of time, you must now pulp them. Do not separate the pulp from the juice, but allow it to stand, covered, for several hours in a cool place (preferably overnight); the cooler the better, as this helps with the precipitation of tannins and the development of the flavor. Now you can press the pulp to extract all the juice. Check the pH, which again will depend on the variety of pear used, but aim for a pH in the range 3.9 to 4.0. To lower the pH add malic acid; to raise it add precipitated chalk. If you want to aid in the clearing of the perry, you can add a pectic enzyme at this stage.

Now check the gravity, aiming for a starting gravity of more than 1.055. Place the juice in a fermenting vessel—a wine fermenter is ideal as this is easy to sanitize. Put the juice under an airlock and leave to ferment naturally. Check the gravity regularly. If you wish to produce a sweet perry, then you should add 1 crushed campden tablet per 5 quarts (5 liters) of juice when your target final gravity is reached. Once this figure is reached, the perry must be matured. Rack the perry into glass carboys and place under an airlock. Cleanliness is of the utmost importance at this stage to avoid the introduction of lactic-acid bacteria, which will produce acetic acid from the natural citric acid of the perry.

Traditionally, perry is left to mature in outbuildings over the winter. The fluctuations in temperature will not harm it, but make sure it doesn't freeze. Once the temperature rises to 60°F (15°C) in the spring or summer, the malolactic fermentation will take place. Once this is finished, the perry can be racked and bottled.

Although the making of perry requires careful attention and a little skill, it is quite possible to make a perry at home that is equal to many of the excellent varieties available in the shops.

GOLDEN PERRY

This recipe produces a golden, semi-dry pear cider, which has the character of a white wine, with a modest pear aroma and flavor. It involves a few more ingredients than the basic perry, but it is worth trying.

Ingredients

2 tsp acid blend
0.3 oz (10 g) champagne yeast
1½ tsp citric acid
2 lb (1 kg) light brown sugar
5 tsp malic acid
19 quarts (18 liters) pear squeezings
1 tsp tannin
3 tsp tartaric acid
4 lb (2 kg) white table sugar

Method

1. Make sure everything has been sanitized.

2. Heat 4 quarts (4 liters) of the pear juice or enough to dissolve the sugars and other ingredients. Stir until the sugar is dissolved.

3. Meanwhile, reconstitute the dried yeast in a cup of warm water (90° to 99°F, 32° to 37°C).

4. When the sugars are dissolved, put the remaining pear juice and pear-juice mixture into a 25-quart (24-liter) carboy, fit a blow-off tube and pitch the yeast. Watch the liquid level in the carboy and top up with fresh pear juice as needed. Fermentation will start to drop off in about 1 month. When it does, rack to a second carboy and top up with fresh pear juice.

5. Wait 45 days before bottling. Sample about 4 months after bottling, but it is better to leave it until it is at least 6 months old as it will mature with age and reach peak flavor.

COUNTRY-STYLE PERRY

If your pear tree is bursting there is only one thing to do with the fruit you can't manage to eat—make perry! For this recipe pears are the only things you need. It is a country-style recipe in which the natural yeast on the fruit is relied upon to ferment the extracted juice. If you don't want to take the chance that there is enough yeast on your fruit, then you can always wash them first and add brewer's yeast to the extracted juice.

Ingredients

Firm, juicy pears, as many as you have

Method

1. Choose your fruit, making sure you avoid any bad or bruised pears.

2. Leave them in a warmish place for several weeks until they are just beginning to soften.

3. Chop and smash the fruit into a pulp.

4. Strain through muslin, pressing very hard so that all juices are extracted. A fruit press is best for this but you may not wish to go to that expense.

5. Keep this juice in a container in a warm place.

6. Allow to bubble.

7. When bubbles rise to the surface of the liquid and the sediment drops to the bottom, put into a cask.

8. Cover the cask tightly and leave for 6 to 7 months.

9. Strain and bottle.

Sloe Gin and Other Infusions

INFUSIONS

Infusing spirits is a great way to experiment with flavors, although you may find it is an ongoing process of tasting, tweaking, then tasting again before you get it right. The basic concept is to combine a variety of flavors into a base liquor, creating a custom-made spirit.

Infusions have been around for centuries and were originally created for medicinal purposes. Mostly herbal in nature, the first infusions were also popular as appetite stimulators consumed before a meal. Driven by consumer demand for one-of-a-kind cocktails, today's infusions include a complete range of flavors from sweet and exotic to savoury and dry.

There is a world of infusions out there but there is nothing to prevent you creating your own appealing drink. Remember that the spirit should not overwhelm the flavors you are working with, so it is important to get the balance right.

Sloe gin is one of the better-known infusions, which uses fruit from the hedgerows. Sloes are the fruit of the blackthorn, a relative of the plum, which are usually ready to harvest by the beginning of September. Sloes produce a rich, red spirit that improves with keeping.

Vodka is the most common base spirit because of its neutral taste, but you can also use many others for infusions. Darker spirits are not so easy to use, as their flavors are usually too strong, but having said that, if you choose the right complementary flavor to the liquid—for example cherry or apricot brandy—then you can end up with an extremely palatable end product. The key to infusions is experimentation. Find out what is going to marry well with the base liquor and build on the flavors.

The advantage of infusions is that you require very little equipment; a large, airtight glass jar is all you need. The other important thing to remember is that the infusion ingredients must be completely submerged in the spirit, so that the flavors are perfectly combined.

Different ingredients will require different steeping times, so follow the guidelines in the recipes in this section and you won't go far wrong. Dried fruits work very well, as you can infuse these longer without the fruit degrading. You don't need to waste the infused fruit, either, as the spirit-soaked dried fruit can be made into a delicious compote, chutney or dessert.

CHOOSING YOUR SPIRIT

When starting out it is a good idea to buy a less expensive spirit so as not to waste money if your experiments go wrong.

CHOOSING YOUR FLAVORS

Herbs, spices, fruits and berries are the most common ingredients for infusions. The most popular infusions are fruit based, but you can use your own imagination to create some innovative combinations.

THE BASICS

Making your own infusions really couldn't be easier. Choose your sterilized, airtight jar. Wash your ingredients, place them inside the jar filled with the spirit. Shake it a few times and cover with the lid.

Store in a cool, dark place and shake it a couple of times a day for the duration of the infusion. Some of the more intense flavors will only need 3 to 4 days, while less intense flavors may need a couple of weeks for the flavors to mature. It is a good idea to taste the infusion every couple of days to see how the flavors are starting to marry and whether you need to add any other ingredients, such as sugar, to the mixture.

Once your infusion has reached its peak, you will need to strain the liquid through a fine strainer or paper coffee filter into another clean jar. Store the finished infusion as you would any other liquor.

PREPARING YOUR INGREDIENTS

Berries

Wash and leave them whole, but score or puncture the skins before immersing them in the spirit.

Pineapple, mango or similar fruit

Wash and cut into chunks.

Strawberries and citrus fruit

Wash and slice thinly or use the zests of lemons and oranges.

Vanilla pods

Wash and cut lengthwise.

Herbs

Wash and use the whole thing, including stems.

Peppers

Wash and leave whole or cut in half.

Garlic

Use whole cloves, removing the outer layers of skin.

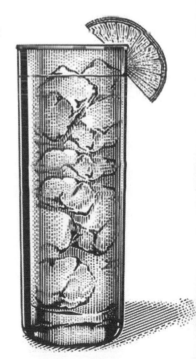

VODKA INFUSIONS

CRANBERRY SPICE INFUSION

Ingredients
    25 fl oz (750 ml) bottle of vodka of
    choice
    3.5 oz (100 g) fresh or frozen cranberries
    5 whole cloves
    1 whole nutmeg, cracked
    1 teaspoon whole coriander seed, cracked
    Half a whole vanilla bean
    Half a stick cinnamon, cracked
    6 whole allspice berries, cracked

Method

1. Place the cranberries and spices in an infusion jar and top with vodka.

2. Leave to infuse for 2 to 3 days, then strain and place infused vodka in an attractive container.

LAVENDER-INFUSED VODKA

This infused vodka adds a floral touch to a vodka martini and makes an ultra refreshing vodka tonic.

Ingredients
    25 fl oz (750 ml) bottle of vodka of
    choice
    1 sprig of rosemary
    2 sprigs of lavender

Method

1. Rinse the herbs and place them in a clean jar with an airtight lid.

2. Pour the vodka over the herbs and shake a few times.

3. Seal the lid tight and store the jar in a dark place for 5 days.

4. Test the flavor of the infusion every day, beginning on the second day.

5. Once the lavender and rosemary flavor is to your taste, strain the herbs from the vodka using a fine strainer or coffee filter.

6. Wash the jar and return the flavored vodka to it.

7. Store as you do other vodka.

GARLIC-INFUSED VODKA

This recipe is a great way to spice up your average vodka and works extremely well in Bloody Marys.

Ingredients
    1 medium-sized bulb of garlic

2 large sprigs of basil
25 fl oz (750 ml) bottle of vodka
of choice

Method

1. Separate the garlic into cloves and remove the skins.

2. Rinse the basil to remove any unwanted chemicals. There is no need to chop or remove the stems.

3. Place the garlic and basil in a clean quart-sized (1 liter) mason Jar. FIll the Jar with vodka.

4. Secure the lid on the jar and shake well.

5. Store the infusion in a dark place at room temperature for 4 days.

6. Strain the vodka through a coffee filter into a separate container.

7. Store as you would any other vodka.

———————

CUCUMBER VODKA

This infusion is fabulously refreshing in summer coolers and martinis.

Ingredients

1 cucumber, sliced (preferably home grown)
25 fl oz (750 ml) bottle of vodka of choice

Method

1. Place the cucumber in a large glass container, add the vodka, and cap tightly.

2. Leave to stand at room temperature for 3 weeks, shaking gently every other day.

3. Taste for the preferred flavor intensity, allowing it to infuse for up to 1 more week if needed. (Do not infuse any longer than 2 weeks, or a bitter flavor will result.)

4. Strain the infused vodka into the original bottle. Cap tightly, label, and refrigerate until ready to serve.

———————

PEPPER VODKA

This spicy boost is guaranteed to produce the best Bloody Marys.

Ingredients

1 serrano chilli, stemmed, seeded and quartered lengthwise
1 jalapeño chilli, stemmed, seeded and quartered lengthwise
1 red habanero chilli, stemmed, seeded and quartered lengthwise
25 fl oz (750 ml) bottle of vodka of choice

Method

1. Place the chillies in a large glass container, add the vodka and cap tightly.

2. Leave to stand at room temperature for 48 hours, shaking gently once or twice a day.

3. Taste for the preferred flavor and heat intensity, leaving it to infuse for up to 2 more days if needed. (Do not infuse any longer than 2 weeks, or a bitter flavor will result.)

4. Strain the infused vodka back into the original bottle. Cap tightly, label and refrigerate until ready to serve.

PINK GRAPEFRUIT VODKA

Fresh grapefruit makes this a refreshing summer cooler.

Ingredients
   1 large pink grapefruit, unpeeled and
      sliced
   25 fl oz (750 ml) bottle of vodka of
      choice

Method
1. Place the grapefruit slices in a large glass container, add the vodka and cap tightly.

2. Leave to stand at room temperature for 1 week, shaking gently every couple of days.

3. Taste for the preferred flavor intensity, allowing it to infuse for up to 1 more week if needed. (Do not infuse any longer than 2 weeks, or a bitter flavor will result.)

4. Strain the infused vodka into the original bottle. Cap tightly, label and refrigerate until ready to serve.

APPLE AND CINNAMON VODKA

This makes a great hot apple cider cocktail.

Ingredients
   4 cinnamon sticks
   6 large red apples
   25 fl oz (750 ml) bottle of vodka of
      choice

Method
1. Slice the apples and toss them into your infusion jar with the cinnamon sticks.

2. Add the vodka and infuse for a few days.

CRANBERRY AND RASPBERRY VODKA

This ruby-colored liqueur makes the ideal Christmas drink or gift.

Method
   1 quart (1 liter) bottle of vodka of choice
   21 oz (600 g) fresh cranberries, roughly
      chopped
   21 oz (600 g) fresh raspberries
   2 lb (900 g) sugar
   4 tablespoons lemon juice

Method

1. Put all the ingredients in a glass container and stir gently until the sugar dissolves. Cover tightly and store in a cupboard for 3 weeks.

2. After 3 weeks, sieve the liqueur into a clean, sterilized container, pressing the fruits through with the back of a wooden spoon. Strain this sieved liquid through double muslin, squeezing the juice from the pulp.

Leave for a couple of hours to allow the sediment to settle.

3. Filter the liquid again, this time through a coffee filter. This could take several hours, so top up the filter whenever you pass by. You may need more than one filter to complete this process. All this is necessary to avoid cloudy liquid. Pour the liqueur into clean bottles.

GIN INFUSIONS

SLOE GIN

Sloe Gin is especially good after a rich meal, as it has great palate-cleansing properties.

Ingredients

  1 lb (450 g) ripe sloes
  0.5 lb (225 g) extra-fine sugar
  1 quart (1 liter) bottle of gin

Method

1. Prick the tough skin of the sloes all over with a clean needle or sharp fork and place in a large sterilized jar.

2. Add the sugar and gin, seal tightly and shake well.

3. Store in a cool, dark cupboard and shake every other day for 1 week. Then shake once a week for 2 months.

4. When ready, strain the liquid through a sieve and place in clean bottles.

5. The sloe gin will now be a beautiful dark red and ready to drink, although it will still improve with keeping.

Tip

Use the steeped sloes to make sloe jelly—delicious served with your Christmas turkey.

BLUEBERRY GIN

There's nothing like a gin and tonic to cool you down on a hot day, but try it with a refreshing blueberry gin instead.

Ingredients

  3.5 oz (100 g) blueberries
  12 tablespoons extra-fine sugar
  25 fl oz (750 ml) bottle of gin of choice

Method

1. Place the blueberries and sugar in a large sterilized jar. Pricking the blueberries first will help bring out their full flavor.

2. Add the gin and shake well. Set aside for at least 2 weeks, shaking the bottle from time to time. This will improve with age, so you can leave the blueberry mixture for up to 2 months before bottling.

3. Strain the liquid through a sieve and pour into clean bottles.

CUCUMBER GIN

Cucumber and gin are a great match—this recipe is quite different and very refreshing.

Ingredients

   25 fl oz (750 ml) bottle of gin of choice
   3 cucumbers, peeled, seeded and diced

Method

1. Place the cucumbers in a large jar or other container with a lid.

2. Add the gin and stir.

3. Set aside in a cool, dark place (the fridge if needed) for 3 days. Stir once every day.

4. Place a fine mesh strainer over a large liquid measuring jug. Strain the cucumber infusion through the strainer and into the measuring jug. Using a spoon or dowel, push as much liquid as possible out of the cucumber and through the strainer.

5. Place a cheesecloth-lined funnel in the original gin bottle. Pour the contents of the measuring jug through the cheesecloth and into the bottle.

6. This liquor will keep for 6 months without refrigeration.

LEMON GIN RECIPE

Ingredients

   1 quart (1 liter) bottle of gin of choice
   7 oz (200 g) white granulated sugar
   3 unwaxed lemons

Method

1. Make space in the gin bottle for the sugar and lemon by pouring off at least 7 fl oz (200 ml) of gin (reserve this).

2. Pare the rind from the lemon, being extra careful to avoid the bitter pith. Add the rind to the bottle.

3. Use a funnel to add the sugar to the gin and shake well. Top up with the reserved gin.

4. Place in a cool, dark place and shake regularly. You can leave it to infuse for as long as you like, as it will only improve.

BRANDY INFUSIONS

CHERRY BRANDY

This simple and delicious drink can be made for Christmas or any other time of year. The recipe is ideal for using up a cheaper brandy that you do not like as much as more expensive brands.

Ingredients

- 2 lb (900 g) Morello cherries, freshly picked and pitted
- 13.5 fl oz (400 ml) bottle of brandy of choice
- 6 oz (170 g) sugar (3.25 oz, 85 g, sugar to every 1 lb, 450 g, cherries)
- A few peach or apricot kernels, or blanched bitter almonds (optional)

Method

1. Have some sterilized glass bottles ready; these must be perfectly dry.

2. Ensure the cherries are not too ripe and are freshly gathered. Cut off about half the stalks.

3. Put them into the bottles, sprinkle the sugar between the cherries and when the bottles are nearly full, pour in enough brandy to reach just below the rim.

4. Add the kernels of almonds now, if using.

5. Seal the bottles to ensure they are airtight and store in a dry place to rest.

6. The brandy will be ready to drink in 2 to 3 months. The cherries will make a perfect topping for ice cream.

APRICOT BRANDY

It takes a few weeks before you can consume this brandy. You will need a wide-necked jar. You get the added bonus of some deliciously preserved boozy apricots. Eat the fruit separately, warmed through and served with brandy snaps and ice cream.

Ingredients

- 12 fresh apricots, washed
- 20 fl oz (591 ml) bottle of brandy of choice
- 0.5 oz (225 g) extra-fine sugar

Method

1. Cut the fruit into small pieces, reserving the pits. Crack open the pits to obtain the kernels and place in the jar with the fruit.

2. Add the brandy and sugar, making sure all the fruit is covered. Seal the jar and shake to dissolve the sugar.

3. Leave in a dark place for 1 month, shaking the jar several times a week.

4. Strain off the fruit and eat separately if desired.

5. Bottle the liqueur and store until required.

BLACKBERRY BRANDY

This is another great hedgerow recipe and makes a delicious alternative to sloe gin.

Ingredients

- 1 lb (450 g) blackberries, freshly picked and washed
- 0.5 lb (225 g) extra-fine sugar
- 1 quart (1 liter) bottle of brandy of choice

Method

1. Place the blackberries in a large, sterilized jar.

2. Pour in the sugar followed by the brandy.

3. Seal the jar tightly and shake well.

4. Store in a cool, dark cupboard and shake every other day for 1 week, then shake once a week for 2 months. The brandy is then ready to drink, but will keep improving if you can manage to leave it longer.

5. When the brandy has steeped for at least 2 months, strain it off into a 1-quart (1-liter) bottle. The brandy is now ready to drink.You can reserve the fruit for a very boozy dessert; a few berries are great served with vanilla ice cream.

PEACH SAKE

This recipe is a very quick and easy-to-make infusion, using sake, the popular Japanese rice wine. As the fruit steeps, it gradually transfers flavor and color to the clear wine, naturally enhancing sake's fruity and floral qualities. You can use almost any fruit, but the recipe here uses peaches.

Ingredients

- 2 to 3 ripe peaches
- 1 quart (1 liter) bottle of sake

Method

1. Cut the peaches in half and remove the pits but not the skins.

2. Slice the peaches thinly, and place in a large sterilized jar.

3. Pour the sake over the peaches, cover and refrigerate for 24 hours.

4. Strain the sake through muslin into a clean decanter, reserving the peaches.

5. Serve immediately, with 3 or 4 peach slices in each glass, or refrigerate the sake and peaches in separate containers to use later. Infused sake will keep for 4 to 5 days in the refrigerator and the peaches will keep for about 3 days.

Non-alcoholic Drinks

SOFT DRINKS

TRADITIONAL LEMONADE

A simple recipe for 1 quart (1 liter) of classic lemonade.

Ingredients

6 unwaxed lemons
25 fl oz (750 ml) water
4.5 oz (125 g) sugar

Method

1. Zest the lemons using a vegetable peeler. Put the zest in a heatproof jug and pour on 10 fl oz (300 ml) boiling water. Stir and set aside for 1 hour.

2. Cut a slice from the center of each lemon and keep to one side. Juice the lemons—you should be able to get about 7 fl oz (200 ml) of fresh lemon juice.

3. Meanwhile put the sugar in a small pan with 3 fl oz (100 ml) water and gently heat until the sugar dissolves. Pour into a large jug and leave to cool.

4. Slowly pour the infused zest water through a sieve into the large jug and discard the zest. Add the freshly squeezed lemon juice, 10 fl oz (300 ml) cold water and some ice cubes. Stir well, add the lemon slices to garnish and serve.

PINK LEMONADE

Pink lemonade has been around since the 19th century. Some commercially made pink lemonades are simply colored with artificial coloring. There are many natural ingredients that can be used to provide the color, some of which may affect the taste. You can use the juice of cherries, red grapefruit, red grapes, cranberries, strawberries or other red fruit juices.

Ingredients

6 unwaxed lemons
25 fl oz (750 ml) water
4.5 oz (125 g) sugar

One of the following coloring agents:
2 tsp grenadine syrup
7 fl oz (200 ml) cranberry juice
or
Juice from a jar of maraschino cherries

Method

1. Follow the method for making traditional lemonade up to the end of step 3.

2. Add the coloring agent when mixing in the lemon juice, cold water and ice to the infused zest water. Garnish with lemon slices before serving.

BLUE LEMONADE

Blue lemonade can be made the same way as pink lemonade, but using 4.5 ounces (125 grams) of blueberries and 4.5 ounces (125 grams) of blackberries puréed in a blender to provide the color. You will need to strain the lemonade well to remove the berry seeds before serving.

FRESH MINT LEMONADE

A refreshing alternative to lemonade.

Ingredients

3.5 oz (100 g) fresh mint
2 quarts (2 liters) water
7 fl oz (200 ml) honey
7 fl oz (200 ml) lemon Juice

Method

1. Finely chop the mint, add to the water in a covered pot and gently heat for 10 minutes. Add the honey, stirring until it dissolves.

2. Remove the pot from heat, cover and leave to cool for several hours or overnight.

3. When the infused water is cool pour through a strainer into a jug, add the lemon juice and chill in the fridge.

LEMON ICED TEA

Ingredients

7 fl oz (200 ml) strong tea
4 fl oz (120 ml) cold water
4 fl oz (120 ml) crushed ice
2 lemons
2 sprigs of fresh mint
Sugar or sweetener to taste

Method

1. Remove a slice from the center of each lemon and set aside. Juice the lemons.

2. Mix the tea, water, lemon juice and sugar or sweetener together in a jug and chill for at least 1 hour in the fridge.

3. Add the ice and garnish with the mint and slices of lemon.

GINGER LEMONADE

A lemonade with a little kick, this drink goes very well with Asian food.

Ingredients

17 fl oz (500 ml) lemon juice (fresh or bottled)
2 quarts (2 liters) water
13 oz (370 g) sugar
7 slices of fresh ginger root

Method

1. Put the water and ginger together in a pot and boil for 5 minutes.

2. Remove from heat, add the lemon juice and sugar and stir until the sugar dissolves.

3. Allow the liquid to cool for about 20 minutes, then remove the ginger root pieces. Chill in a fridge before serving.

For a stronger ginger flavor, chop the ginger into smaller pieces but make sure to strain the lemonade well before serving.

LAVENDER LEMONADE

A lemonade with the floral aroma of lavender: summer in a glass.

Ingredients

    6 unwaxed lemons
    25 fl oz (750 ml) water
    4.5 oz (125 g) sugar
    18 oz (500 g) lavender leaves, chopped

Method

Follow the recipe for making traditional lemonade but add the lavender with the lemon zest to infuse in the boiling water.

MIDDLE EASTERN LEMONADE

Middle Eastern lemonade is a little different from the traditional Western lemonade. Middle Eastern lemonade is not supposed to be sweet but you can add more sugar if you wish.

Ingredients

    Juice of 3 lemons
    Juice of 6 limes
    7 oz (200 g) granulated sugar
    1 tsp orange blossom water
    1.75 oz (50 g) fresh mint, finely chopped
    1 quart (1 liter) cold water
    Crushed ice

Method

1. In a blender, blend the water, orange blossom water, lemon and lime juice and mint.

2. Chill in a fridge. Pour into glasses filled with crushed ice and serve.

TRADITIONAL GINGER BEER

Ginger beer was first produced in Britain as an alcoholic beverage in the 18th century. Britain could export ginger beer because of the quality of the stoneware bottles in which it was stored. It is still popular in many regions influenced by the British Empire, including the Caribbean, East Africa and Corfu.

Today ginger beer is almost always produced as a soft drink.

Ingredients
  1 lb (450 g) sugar
  5 quarts (5 liters) water
  1 unwaxed lemon
  1.5 oz (40 g) root ginger
  0.75 oz (25 g) cream of tartar
  0.75 oz (25 g) brewers yeast

Also needed
Clean, sanitized plastic fizzy drinks bottles. **Do not use glass bottles because of the risk of these exploding.**

Method
1. Bruise the ginger to release the flavor (mash it with a rolling pin but don't crush it).

2. Peel the lemon, (leaving the pith on) and squeeze the juice.

3. Place the ginger, lemon rind and cream of tartar into a large bowl. Add the boiling water and lemon juice and stir well.

4. Allow the mixture to cool to about 70°F (21°C), remove 3 fl oz (100 ml) of the liquid and mix with the yeast. Stir the yeast mixture back into the liquid.

5. Cover the bowl with a clean cloth and leave in a dark, warm place (66 to 73°F, 19 to 23°C) for 24 hours.

6. Strain the liquid through a fine cloth into another bowl. Allow the sediment to settle, then siphon the liquid into the bottles.

7. Keep the bottles in a warm, dark place (66 to 73°F, 19 to 23°C) for 12 to 24 hours.

You can judge how well the bottles are carbonated by gently squeezing the sides of the bottles, unscrew the cap a little if the pressure gets excessive. You may wish to store the bottles in a covered bucket, as there is a small chance they could leak or explode.

8. Move the beer to a cool place and it will be ready to drink after 2 to 3 days. Chill before drinking.

GINGER ALE

Ingredients
  1.5 oz (40 g) fresh ginger, finely grated
  6 oz (170 g) sugar
  2 quarts (2 liters) water
  ¼ tsp brewers yeast
  2 Tbsp lemon juice

Also needed:
Clean, sanitized 2-quart (2-liter) plastic bottle.

Method
1. Place the ginger, sugar, and 4 fl oz (125 ml) of the water into a large saucepan and heat gently. Stir until the sugar has dissolved.

2. Remove from the heat, cover and allow to steep for 1 hour.

3. Pour the infused syrup through a fine strainer set over a bowl, pressing the pulp to get all of the juice out of the mixture.

4. Chill the syrup quickly by placing in the fridge.

5. Using a funnel, pour the syrup into the bottle and add the yeast, lemon juice and remaining water.

6. Place the cap on the bottle, gently shake and leave the bottle at 66 to 73°F (19 to 23°C) for 48 hours. Unscrew the cap a little if the pressure gets excessive.

7. Store in the fridge for up to 2 weeks.

————••••••••••————

COLA DRINK

The recipes of the big cola companies are a closely guarded secret. It is believed that the original recipes contained sugar, caffeine, caramel, phosphoric acid, decocainized coca leaf, kola nuts, lime, glycerine and vanilla extract as the main ingredients. Flavorings used may have included lemon oil, lavender oil, orange oil, neroli oil, cassia oil, nutmeg oil and coriander oil. This is a simpler recipe for making at home. This is also safer, as using kola nuts, coca leaf, essential oils and phosphoric acid can all be hazardous.

Ingredients
Zest of 2 oranges
Zest of 2 limes
Zest of 1 lemon
1 tsp ground cinnamon
1 tsp ground nutmeg
1 tsp ground star anise
½ tsp dried lavender flowers
0.3 oz (10 g) stem ginger
A third of a vanilla pod with the seeds
  scraped out and added as well
¼ teaspoon citric acid
10.5 oz (300 g) extra-fine sugar
2 tsp brown sugar
2 Tbsp caramel color

Method
1. Add all of the ingredients apart from the sugars to 17 fl oz (500 ml) of water, bring to the boil, then let it simmer for 20 to 30 minutes.

2. Strain this infusion through a sieve into a large bowl while it is still hot.

3. After straining stir in the extra-fine and brown sugar and the caramel coloring.

4. You now have a syrup that you can dilute at a ratio of 1 parts syrup to 4 pars soda water.

————••••••••••————

ELDERFLOWER CORDIAL

Elderflowers are plentiful in the summer; here is a recipe to capture their delicate flavor.

Ingredients

- 25–30 elderflower heads
- 2 quarts (2 liters) cold water
- 3 lb (1.25 kg) sugar
- 3 tsp citric acid
- 3 lemons thinly sliced

Method

1. Mix all the ingredients together in a plastic bucket.

2. Leave in a cool, dark place for 24 to 48 hours, stirring occasionally.

3. Strain into bottles, store in fridge and dilute before use.

This cordial can be kept frozen in suitable containers.

———

COFFEE FRAPPÉ

Ingredients

- 18–22 ice cubes, crushed
- 8 fl oz (250 ml) espresso-strength coffee, chilled
- 4 tablespoons granulated sugar
- 4 tablespoons flavored syrup of choice (optional)
- Whipped cream, to garnish

Method

Place the ice, coffee, sugar and syrup in a blender. Blend until the frappe is smooth. Pour into a large, tall glass. Garnish with a dollop of whipped cream.

———

STRAWBERRY CORDIAL

Ingredients

- 1 quart (1 liter) strawberries (fully ripe)
- Juice of 1 lemon
- Juice of 1 orange
- 1.5 quarts (1.5 liters) water
- 1 lb (450 g) sugar

Method

1. Mash the strawberries through a sieve. Add the juice of the lemon and orange, then add the water and mix thoroughly.

2. Leave to stand for 2 hours.

3. Put the sugar into a bowl and strain the juice over it, stirring until the sugar has completely dissolved.

4. Served with ice this makes a delicious, refreshing drink on a hot summer's day.

———

HANGOVER CURES

Prevention is better than cure; if you don't want to suffer a hangover, don't drink, or if you do, drink in moderation. Having said that, there are things you can do to avoid hangovers or to lessen the effect of a hangover.

Many people believe that there is more chance of suffering a hangover if you drink homemade wine or beer. In fact the opposite may be the case. Homebrew is not usually filtered to the same extent as commercially made drinks. This means that they will usually contain a small amount of yeast and this yeast is high in B vitamins, which are depleted in your body by alcohol consumption. B vitamins are essential to alcohol metabolism and therefore may lessen the effects of a hangover.

Vitamin C also helps deal with the alcohol, so drink a glass of orange juice.

Don't drink on an empty stomach; food will help slow the body's absorption of the alcohol.

Drink plenty of water or soft drinks in between alcoholic drinks and try to drink as much water as you can after a night on the town. If you drink tea or coffee this may also dehydrate you further, so keep up with the water to counteract this.

Avoid salt as it tends to maximize the process of dehydration. Non-fizzy sports drinks contain vitamins and are ideal for rehydration.

If you need a painkiller a soluble aspirin in water is best.

The following remedies have been claimed to work but come with no guarantees:

A popular cure is the prairie oyster, which is a raw egg, with yolk intact, with 2 dashes of vinegar and a teaspoon each of Worcestershire sauce, tomato ketchup and tabasco. Drink in one swig.

A Sicilian folk remedy was to eat dried bull penis. The ancient Romans ate cabbage leaves, while the Egyptians drank cabbage water.

The cowboys of the Wild West drank rabbit-dropping tea.

Germans swear by herring with mustard. In Outer Mongolia they eat pickled sheep eyes in tomato juice.

Beetroot juice is something else you can try because it is supposed to cleanse the liver and cleanse your entire system of the toxic effects of alcohol.

Celery is a great source of calcium and magnesium both of which are supposed to have a calming effect on the central nervous system.

Spinach is highly cleansing and is essential for the body's circulatory system, especially to the brain, so why not boost the brain cells with a breakfast of poached egg on top of some spinach.

BREAKFAST IN A GLASS

This recipe contains many of the components of a good hangover cure. Prepare before a night out on the town.

Ingredients
(Serves 2)

- 1.25 oz (35 g) porridge oats
- 5 fl oz (150 ml) skimmed milk
- 1 large cooking apple
- 1 orange
- 5 fl oz (150 ml) buttermilk
- 2 tablespoons honey
- 1 egg

Method

1. Put the porridge oats and skimmed milk in a bowl, cover and leave to soak overnight in the fridge.

2. Peel, core and chop the apple. Grate the rind off the orange, then juice it. Put the apple chunks, orange rind and orange juice into a small saucepan, bring to the boil and simmer for 10 minutes, or until the apple is tender. Set aside to cool, then chill overnight.

3. The following morning put the porridge oats, milk, apple, buttermilk, honey and egg in a blender and liquidize.

4. Divide the drink between 2 glasses.

HANGOVER SMOOTHIE

This tastes great and is good at helping to soothe the hammering in your head.

Ingredients
- Half a banana
- ½ cup of milk
- 2 tablespoons honey
- 2 scoops frozen yogurt or vanilla ice cream

Method

Put all the ingredients in a blender—f your head can stand the noise—and enjoy.

If all of the above remedies fail you could try some voodoo and stick 13 pins into the cork of the bottle that did the damage!

GLOSSARY

ABV: Alcohol by volume—a worldwide, standard measure of how much alcohol is contained in an alcoholic beverage.

All grain: Alternative term for full mash.

Acetification: The conversion of alcohol into vinegar.

Ale: A class of beer made with a top fermenting yeast that is fermented at warm temperatures.

Alpha acid: Alpha acids are the hop components that contribute to the bitterness of beer.

Aroma hops: Hops, usually low in *alpha acids* but high in essential oils, added in the last few minutes of the boil to provide flavor and aroma.

Attenuation: The decrease in original gravity that occurs as the fermentation process converts sugars to alcohol.

Base malt: A *malt* such as pale malt that is used in a beer to provide the main sugar source for fermentation.

Bentonite: A *fining agent* made from an American clay.

Bittering hops: Hops added at or near the beginning of the boil to provide bitterness.

Campden tablet: A sanitizer commonly used in wine making to prevent the growth of unwanted yeast and bacteria.

Carboy: A large glass vessel used by home brewers for fermenting beer or wine. Usually 20 to 24 quarts (19 or 23 liters) in size.

Cold break: Term used for the process of, and the material formed, when proteins coagulate and drop out of the *wort* when it is cooled rapidly after the boil.

Conditioning: The process of carbonating beer.

DME: Abbreviation for dry malt extract.

Dry hopping: Adding hops after the boiling process to provide hop aroma and flavor but not bitterness.

Enzyme: A protein capable of breaking or forming chemical bonds in organic substances.

Fermenter: A container in which fermentation takes place, usually made of glass or food-grade plastic.

Final gravity: The density of a liquid after fermentation has taken place.

Fining agent: A substance used to clarify beer or wine (e.g. Irish moss).

Flavor hops: Hops added within the last 20 minutes of the boil to provide flavor and some aroma to the beer.

Flocculation: In brewing, this refers to the clumping together of yeast cells and/or proteins to form larger particles that drop out of the *wort* quickly. Higher flocculation means clearer beer.

Gelatin: A beer and wine *fining agent* made from animal products.

Grist: The mixture of crushed grains used in a mash.

Isinglass: A *fining agent* made from the swim bladders of sturgeon fish.

Headspace: The space at the top of a fermenting vessel that does not contain liquid. Headspace should be minimized in the secondary fermenter to prevent oxidation but is not a concern in a primary because carbon dioxide from fermentation protects the *wort* or *must*.

Hot break: The coagulation and dropping out of proteins during *wort* boiling.

Hydrometer: A device that measures the density of liquid in comparison to the density of pure water. One can determine the alcohol content of a finished beer or wine by comparing the original gravity and final gravity.

Irish moss: A seaweed used to clarify beer.

Krausen: (kroy-zen) The foam that grows on top of *wort* as it ferments.

Krausening: A method of carbonating beer by adding fermenting *wort* (i.e. *wort* with a *krausen*) to a fermented batch just before it is bottled.

Lager: A class of beer made with a bottom fermenting yeast strain. Usually fermented at cooler temperatures than ale and lagered (stored cold) after fermentation.

Lees: The sediment made of dead yeast cells and fruit pulp at the bottom of wine that has been left to settle.

LME: Abbreviation for liquid malt extract.

Lovibond: A measure of the color of malts and beers. The higher the lovibond, the darker the color.

Malt: Usually refers to malted barley or any grain that has undergone the malting process.

Malt extract: Condensed/concentrated *wort* available in either a liquid or dry form.

Mash: Process in which crushed, malted grains are soaked with hot water, which causes enzymes to convert the starches in to sugars.

Must: The liquid made from crushed or pulped fruit and sometimes other ingredients, such as sugar and flowers, that is used to make wine.

Original gravity: The density of the *wort* or *must* before fermentation occurs.

Oxidation: The effect of oxygen on beer and wine, which causes a stale taste and aroma. In most cases oxidation is unwanted, except in sherry and some strong, dark ales.

Pectic enzyme: A compound added to wine must to prevent pectin hazes.

Pitch: The adding of yeast to the *wort* or *must.*

Pomace: In winemaking, the pulp, skins and seeds that remain after the liquid has been removed.

Punch down: To break up the cap and mix the skins and pulp into the *must.*

Priming: The addition of sugar to finished beer to condition the beer in the bottle.

Rack: To siphon liquid off a sediment into another vessel.

Skunking: A reaction between ultra-violet light and hop compounds that causes beer to smell "skunky."

Sparging: Rinsing sugars from the grain with hot water after mashing.

Specialty malt: Any malt used in small quantities in the mash to impart flavor, color or aroma rather than fermentable sugars. Most specialty grains do not need to be mashed and can be steeped.

Steeping: The process of soaking grains in water to extract color, flavor, aroma or body. There is no starch-to-sugar conversion, as this occurs during *mashing.*

Tannin: The phenolic compounds responsible for astringent and bitter flavors.

Wort: Pronounced "wert." The liquid resulting from the washing and boiling processes.

INDEX